Grade 3

Addison-Wesley Mathematics

Practice Workbook

D1406700

▲▼Addison-Wesley Publishing Company

Menlo Park, California ▪ *Reading, Massachusetts* ▪ *New York*
Don Mills, Ontario ▪ *Wokingham, England* ▪ *Amsterdam* ▪ *Bonn*
Sydney ▪ *Singapore* ▪ *Tokyo* ▪ *Madrid* ▪ *San Juan*

ISBN 0-201-27303-9

4 5 6 7 8 9 10 - HC - 95 94 93 92 91

Table of Contents

Understanding Addition and Subtraction

Show each action, compare or find the missing part using counters.
Complete the number sentence.

1.

3 caterpillars sit on a rock. 3
more caterpillars join them.
How many caterpillars in all?

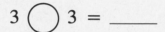

3 ◯ 3 = _____

2.

2 birds sit on a wire. 7 more
birds fly to the wire. How
many birds are on the wire?

2 ◯ 7 = _____

3.

5 spiders move on a web. 2
crawl off. How many are left
on the web?

5 ◯ 2 = _____

4.

4 ducks swim in the water. 2
ducks sit on a log. How many
more ducks are in the water?

4 ◯ 2 = _____

5.

8 worms crawl to 3 apples. Each
worm wants an apple. How
many worms do not get apples?

8 ◯ 3 = ___

6.

There are flowers for 6 bees. 2
bees find flowers. How many
more bees can find flowers?

6 ◯ 2 = ___

Name _____

Counting On and Counting Back

Add or subtract.

1. $9 - 1 =$ _____ **2.** $4 + 1 =$ _____ **3.** $6 - 0 =$ _____

4. $2 + 6 =$ _____ **5.** $10 - 2 =$ _____ **6.** $8 + 2 =$ _____

7. $8 - 1 =$ _____ **8.** $12 - 3 =$ _____ **9.** $3 + 7 =$ _____

10. $\begin{array}{r} 1 \\ +5 \\ \hline \end{array}$ **11.** $\begin{array}{r} 2 \\ +8 \\ \hline \end{array}$ **12.** $\begin{array}{r} 12 \\ -2 \\ \hline \end{array}$ **13.** $\begin{array}{r} 7 \\ -0 \\ \hline \end{array}$ **14.** $\begin{array}{r} 2 \\ +7 \\ \hline \end{array}$

15. $\begin{array}{r} 6 \\ -2 \\ \hline \end{array}$ **16.** $\begin{array}{r} 11 \\ -3 \\ \hline \end{array}$ **17.** $\begin{array}{r} 2 \\ +9 \\ \hline \end{array}$ **18.** $\begin{array}{r} 1 \\ +7 \\ \hline \end{array}$ **19.** $\begin{array}{r} 3 \\ +8 \\ \hline \end{array}$

20. $\begin{array}{r} 7 \\ -3 \\ \hline \end{array}$ **21.** $\begin{array}{r} 0 \\ +6 \\ \hline \end{array}$ **22.** $\begin{array}{r} 10 \\ -1 \\ \hline \end{array}$ **23.** $\begin{array}{r} 3 \\ +9 \\ \hline \end{array}$ **24.** $\begin{array}{r} 6 \\ -3 \\ \hline \end{array}$

25. Find the sum of 8 and 3. _____ **26.** Subtract 3 from 7. _____

27. Subtract 0 from 8. _____ **28.** Find the sum of 6 and 3. _____

Finding Sums

Add.

1. $4 + 4 =$ _____ **2.** $6 + 6 =$ _____ **3.** $5 + 4 =$ _____

4. $2 + 2 =$ _____ **5.** $9 + 8 =$ _____ **6.** $5 + 6 =$ _____

7. $6 + 7 =$ _____ **8.** $7 + 7 =$ _____ **9.** $3 + 4 =$ _____

10. $9 + 9 =$ _____ **11.** $8 + 9 =$ _____ **12.** $5 + 6 =$ _____

13. $\begin{array}{r} 8 \\ + 8 \\ \hline \end{array}$ **14.** $\begin{array}{r} 4 \\ + 5 \\ \hline \end{array}$ **15.** $\begin{array}{r} 2 \\ + 5 \\ \hline \end{array}$ **16.** $\begin{array}{r} 6 \\ + 5 \\ \hline \end{array}$ **17.** $\begin{array}{r} 6 \\ + 3 \\ \hline \end{array}$

18. $\begin{array}{r} 3 \\ + 4 \\ \hline \end{array}$ **19.** $\begin{array}{r} 2 \\ + 6 \\ \hline \end{array}$ **20.** $\begin{array}{r} 7 \\ + 1 \\ \hline \end{array}$ **21.** $\begin{array}{r} 9 \\ + 8 \\ \hline \end{array}$ **22.** $\begin{array}{r} 2 \\ + 8 \\ \hline \end{array}$

23. $\begin{array}{r} 3 \\ + 3 \\ \hline \end{array}$ **24.** $\begin{array}{r} 1 \\ + 7 \\ \hline \end{array}$ **25.** $\begin{array}{r} 7 \\ + 2 \\ \hline \end{array}$ **26.** $\begin{array}{r} 8 \\ + 3 \\ \hline \end{array}$ **27.** $\begin{array}{r} 8 \\ + 7 \\ \hline \end{array}$

28. $\begin{array}{r} 5 \\ + 5 \\ \hline \end{array}$ **29.** $\begin{array}{r} 3 \\ + 2 \\ \hline \end{array}$ **30.** $\begin{array}{r} 7 \\ + 3 \\ \hline \end{array}$ **31.** $\begin{array}{r} 8 \\ + 6 \\ \hline \end{array}$ **32.** $\begin{array}{r} 2 \\ + 4 \\ \hline \end{array}$

Finding Sums

Add.

1. $8 + 3 =$ _____   **2.** $4 + 7 =$ _____   **3.** $7 + 7 =$ _____

4. $9 + 7 =$ _____   **5.** $6 + 4 =$ _____   **6.** $5 + 9 =$ _____

7. $4 + 4 =$ _____   **8.** $3 + 9 =$ _____   **9.** $6 + 6 =$ _____

10. $4 + 6 =$ _____   **11.** $9 + 2 =$ _____   **12.** $6 + 1 =$ _____

13. $\begin{array}{r} 8 \\ + 5 \\ \hline \end{array}$ **14.** $\begin{array}{r} 7 \\ + 6 \\ \hline \end{array}$ **15.** $\begin{array}{r} 8 \\ + 4 \\ \hline \end{array}$ **16.** $\begin{array}{r} 7 \\ + 4 \\ \hline \end{array}$ **17.** $\begin{array}{r} 4 \\ + 3 \\ \hline \end{array}$

18. $\begin{array}{r} 9 \\ + 3 \\ \hline \end{array}$ **19.** $\begin{array}{r} 9 \\ + 9 \\ \hline \end{array}$ **20.** $\begin{array}{r} 3 \\ + 3 \\ \hline \end{array}$ **21.** $\begin{array}{r} 8 \\ + 6 \\ \hline \end{array}$ **22.** $\begin{array}{r} 9 \\ + 6 \\ \hline \end{array}$

23. $\begin{array}{r} 7 \\ + 5 \\ \hline \end{array}$ **24.** $\begin{array}{r} 3 \\ + 8 \\ \hline \end{array}$ **25.** $\begin{array}{r} 3 \\ + 7 \\ \hline \end{array}$ **26.** $\begin{array}{r} 8 \\ + 7 \\ \hline \end{array}$ **27.** $\begin{array}{r} 4 \\ + 8 \\ \hline \end{array}$

28. Find the sum of 6 and 8. _____

29. Find the sum of 9 and 1. _____

30. Find the sum of 5 and 6. _____

Addition and Subtraction

Add or subtract.

1. $6 + 3 =$ _____   **2.** $7 - 4 =$ _____   **3.** $6 - 1 =$ _____

4. $9 + 4 =$ _____   **5.** $4 + 4 =$ _____   **6.** $0 + 7 =$ _____

7. $9 - 4 =$ _____   **8.** $8 - 2 =$ _____

9. $\begin{array}{r} 6 \\ + 6 \\ \hline \end{array}$ **10.** $\begin{array}{r} 7 \\ + 6 \\ \hline \end{array}$ **11.** $\begin{array}{r} 9 \\ + 9 \\ \hline \end{array}$ **12.** $\begin{array}{r} 8 \\ + 9 \\ \hline \end{array}$ **13.** $\begin{array}{r} 9 \\ - 2 \\ \hline \end{array}$

14. $\begin{array}{r} 0 \\ + 5 \\ \hline \end{array}$ **15.** $\begin{array}{r} 7 \\ + 7 \\ \hline \end{array}$ **16.** $\begin{array}{r} 6 \\ - 3 \\ \hline \end{array}$ **17.** $\begin{array}{r} 10 \\ - 6 \\ \hline \end{array}$ **18.** $\begin{array}{r} 5 \\ + 9 \\ \hline \end{array}$

19. $\begin{array}{r} 8 \\ - 5 \\ \hline \end{array}$ **20.** $\begin{array}{r} 5 \\ + 6 \\ \hline \end{array}$ **21.** $\begin{array}{r} 9 \\ - 3 \\ \hline \end{array}$ **22.** $\begin{array}{r} 1 \\ + 8 \\ \hline \end{array}$ **23.** $\begin{array}{r} 9 \\ + 4 \\ \hline \end{array}$

Complete the number sentences.

24. A pet store has 10 chicks. The store owner sold 7. How many are left?

$$10 \bigcirc 7 = \text{\_\_\_\_}$$

25. A family's cat has 6 kittens. 2 are gray. The rest are white. How many are white?

$$6 \bigcirc 2 = \text{\_\_\_\_}$$

26. Juan's team is 2 points ahead of Sally's team. Sally's team has a score of 10. What score does Juan's team have?

$$10 \bigcirc 2 = \text{\_\_\_\_}$$

27. Matt's team has 8 points. They score 3 more points. What is their score?

$$8 \bigcirc 3 = \text{\_\_\_\_}$$

Name _____

Finding Differences

Subtract.

1. $13 - 4 =$ _____   **2.** $9 - 6 =$ _____   **3.** $10 - 9 =$ _____

4. $17 - 8 =$ _____   **5.** $14 - 6 =$ _____   **6.** $9 - 2 =$ _____

7. $15 - 7 =$ _____   **8.** $12 - 9 =$ _____   **9.** $6 - 3 =$ _____

10. $15 - 8 =$ _____   **11.** $14 - 8 =$ _____   **12.** $12 - 3 =$ _____

13. $\begin{array}{r}13\\-\ 5\\\hline\end{array}$	**14.** $\begin{array}{r}9\\-\ 6\\\hline\end{array}$	**15.** $\begin{array}{r}15\\-\ 7\\\hline\end{array}$	**16.** $\begin{array}{r}16\\-\ 7\\\hline\end{array}$	**17.** $\begin{array}{r}12\\-\ 4\\\hline\end{array}$
18. $\begin{array}{r}14\\-\ 6\\\hline\end{array}$	**19.** $\begin{array}{r}11\\-\ 7\\\hline\end{array}$	**20.** $\begin{array}{r}11\\-\ 6\\\hline\end{array}$	**21.** $\begin{array}{r}12\\-\ 8\\\hline\end{array}$	**22.** $\begin{array}{r}10\\-\ 7\\\hline\end{array}$
23. $\begin{array}{r}12\\-\ 6\\\hline\end{array}$	**24.** $\begin{array}{r}9\\-\ 3\\\hline\end{array}$	**25.** $\begin{array}{r}10\\-\ 8\\\hline\end{array}$	**26.** $\begin{array}{r}15\\-\ 6\\\hline\end{array}$	**27.** $\begin{array}{r}11\\-\ 8\\\hline\end{array}$
28. $\begin{array}{r}17\\-\ 9\\\hline\end{array}$	**29.** $\begin{array}{r}18\\-\ 9\\\hline\end{array}$	**30.** $\begin{array}{r}13\\-\ 9\\\hline\end{array}$	**31.** $\begin{array}{r}16\\-\ 8\\\hline\end{array}$	**32.** $\begin{array}{r}12\\-\ 7\\\hline\end{array}$
33. $\begin{array}{r}9\\-\ 7\\\hline\end{array}$	**34.** $\begin{array}{r}15\\-\ 9\\\hline\end{array}$	**35.** $\begin{array}{r}7\\-\ 4\\\hline\end{array}$	**36.** $\begin{array}{r}14\\-\ 9\\\hline\end{array}$	**37.** $\begin{array}{r}12\\-\ 5\\\hline\end{array}$

Name _____

Finding Differences

Subtract.

1. $17 - 8 =$ _____   **2.** $9 - 4 =$ _____   **3.** $13 - 4 =$ _____

4. $14 - 8 =$ _____   **5.** $10 - 6 =$ _____   **6.** $8 - 8 =$ _____

7. $10 - 7 =$ _____   **8.** $15 - 9 =$ _____   **9.** $16 - 8 =$ _____

10. $11 - 7 =$ _____   **11.** $7 - 5 =$ _____   **12.** $18 - 9 =$ _____

13. $\begin{array}{r} 14 \\ -\ 6 \\ \hline \end{array}$ **14.** $\begin{array}{r} 15 \\ -\ 8 \\ \hline \end{array}$ **15.** $\begin{array}{r} 13 \\ -\ 9 \\ \hline \end{array}$ **16.** $\begin{array}{r} 10 \\ -\ 7 \\ \hline \end{array}$ **17.** $\begin{array}{r} 5 \\ -\ 5 \\ \hline \end{array}$

18. $\begin{array}{r} 14 \\ -\ 6 \\ \hline \end{array}$ **19.** $\begin{array}{r} 9 \\ -\ 4 \\ \hline \end{array}$ **20.** $\begin{array}{r} 12 \\ -\ 3 \\ \hline \end{array}$ **21.** $\begin{array}{r} 12 \\ -\ 4 \\ \hline \end{array}$ **22.** $\begin{array}{r} 12 \\ -\ 7 \\ \hline \end{array}$

23. $\begin{array}{r} 11 \\ -\ 6 \\ \hline \end{array}$ **24.** $\begin{array}{r} 13 \\ -\ 6 \\ \hline \end{array}$ **25.** $\begin{array}{r} 11 \\ -\ 5 \\ \hline \end{array}$ **26.** $\begin{array}{r} 6 \\ -\ 6 \\ \hline \end{array}$ **27.** $\begin{array}{r} 12 \\ -\ 8 \\ \hline \end{array}$

28. $\begin{array}{r} 10 \\ -\ 2 \\ \hline \end{array}$ **29.** $\begin{array}{r} 11 \\ -\ 8 \\ \hline \end{array}$ **30.** $\begin{array}{r} 10 \\ -\ 8 \\ \hline \end{array}$ **31.** $\begin{array}{r} 9 \\ -\ 7 \\ \hline \end{array}$ **32.** $\begin{array}{r} 8 \\ -\ 0 \\ \hline \end{array}$

33. $\begin{array}{r} 13 \\ -\ 8 \\ \hline \end{array}$ **34.** $\begin{array}{r} 15 \\ -\ 9 \\ \hline \end{array}$ **35.** $\begin{array}{r} 10 \\ -\ 4 \\ \hline \end{array}$ **36.** $\begin{array}{r} 12 \\ -\ 5 \\ \hline \end{array}$ **37.** $\begin{array}{r} 14 \\ -\ 7 \\ \hline \end{array}$

Fact Families

Find the sums and differences.

1.

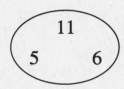

Fact Family Numbers

5	6	11	11
+ 6	+ 5	− 5	− 6

2.

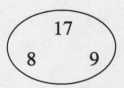

Fact Family Numbers

8	9	17	17
+ 9	+ 8	− 8	− 9

3. 8 +6

4. 5 +7

5. 4 +4

6. 6 +4

7. 9 +7

8. 14 − 6

9. 12 − 7

10. 8 − 4

11. 10 − 4

12. 16 − 7

13. 3 +8

14. 3 +2

15. 6 +9

16. 4 +1

17. 5 +5

18. 11 − 8

19. 5 −2

20. 15 − 9

21. 5 −1

22. 10 − 5

Sums with Three Addends

Look for sums of 10. Write the sums.

Time yourself. Time: _____ minutes.

1.   6
      3
  + 7
_____

2.   2
      6
  + 4
_____

3.   3
      5
  + 5
_____

4.   7
      3
  + 4
_____

5.   4
      7
  + 6
_____

6.   1
      2
  + 6
_____

7.   7
      5
  + 3
_____

8.   3
      2
  + 4
_____

9.   4
      6
  + 3
_____

10.   8
      2
  + 6
_____

11.   5
      2
  + 5
_____

12.   8
      1
  + 9
_____

13.   4
      3
  + 6
_____

14.   5
      4
  + 5
_____

15.   1
      0
  + 9
_____

16.   7
      1
  + 5
_____

17.   8
      0
  + 3
_____

18.   4
      3
  + 1
_____

19.   9
      3
  + 1
_____

20.   5
      7
  + 2
_____

21. $6 + 7 + 3 =$ ___   **22.** $2 + 8 + 8 =$ ___   **23.** $1 + 6 + 2 =$ ___

24. $3 + 4 + 1 =$ ___   **25.** $2 + 9 + 1 =$ ___   **26.** $8 + 3 + 7 =$ ___

Now use a calculator and time yourself again. **Answers will vary.**

Time: _____ minutes.

Which way took longer? _____ Which way was better for you? _____

Problem Solving: Introduction

Choose the number sentence you could use to solve the problem. Do not solve.

1. Before a concert, 237 tickets were sold. At the door, 167 tickets were sold. How many tickets were sold in all?

      A. 237 + 167

      B. 237 − 167

2. The school auditorium has 540 seats. During the concert, 23 seats were empty. How many seats were filled?

      A. 540 + 23

      B. 540 − 23

3. A flute costs $310. A piccolo costs $220. How much for both instruments?

      A. $310 + $220

      B. $310 − $220

4. A trumpet costs $450. A trombone costs $430. How much more for the trumpet?

      A. $450 + $430

      B. $450 − $430

Solve.

5. The school chorus has 15 girls and 24 boys. How many children are in the chorus?

6. In the school band, 7 children play flute. The band has 37 members. How many children play other instruments?

7. The chorus sang for 20 minutes. The band played for 24 minutes. How long did the concert last?

8. Luis practiced his solo for 27 minutes. Arliss practiced her solo for 21 minutes. How much longer did Luis practice?

Name _____

Reading and Writing Numbers

Tell how many hundreds, tens, and ones.
Then write the number.

1.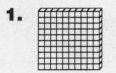

_____ hundreds

_____ tens

_____ ones

_____

2.

_____ hundreds

_____ tens

_____ ones

_____

3.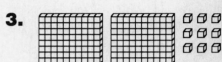

_____ hundreds

_____ tens

_____ ones

_____

Draw pictures of place-value models for each number.
Then write the number.

4. seventy-four

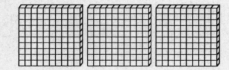

_____

5. one hundred six

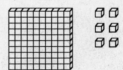

_____

6. three hundred

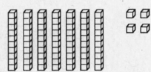

_____

7. two hundred fifty-five

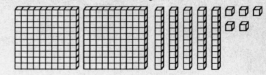

_____

8. Write the numbers in which the 7 has the value 70.

576   721   472   807   799   370   671   704

_____   _____   _____

Counting and Order

Write the number of the next page.

1.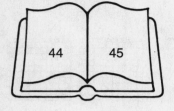

44   45

_____

2.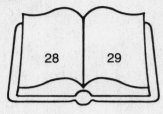

28   29

_____

3.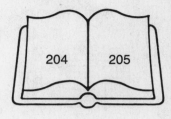

204   205

_____

4.

278   279

_____

5.

138   139

_____

6.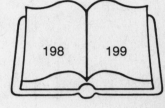

198   199

_____

Write the number that comes after.

7. 45 _____   **8.** 299 _____   **9.** 384 _____   **10.** 469 _____

11. 18 _____   **12.** 49 _____   **13.** 60 _____   **14.** 699 _____

Write the number that comes before.

15. 728 _____   **16.** 100 _____   **17.** 97 _____   **18.** 311 _____

19. 444 _____   **20.** 21 _____   **21.** 80 _____   **22.** 351 _____

23. 54 _____   **24.** 110 _____   **25.** 400 _____   **26.** 297 _____

Skip Counting Patterns

Number Patterns

A   22, 24, 26, 28, . . .
B   35, 40, 45, 50, . . .
C   121, 221, 321, 421, . . .
D   8, 10, 12, 14, . . .
E   72, 82, 92, 102, . . .
F   45, 145, 245, 345, . . .
G   120, 130, 140, 150, . . .
H   185, 190, 195, 200, . . .

Write the letter that matches each pattern.
There can be more than one letter for each pattern.

1. Counting by 2s _____

2. Counting by 10s _____

3. Counting by 5s _____

4. Counting by 100s _____

Give the next four numbers for each pattern.

5. Pattern B _____, _____, _____, _____

6. Pattern D _____, _____, _____, _____

7. Pattern C _____, _____, _____, _____

Write the letters that use these patterns.

8. all even numbers _____

9. all odd numbers _____

10. both even and odd numbers _____

Draw a Picture

Draw a picture to help you solve each problem.

1. In the line for lunch, Mark stood behind Amy. Kate stood behind Mark. Sato stood between Mark and Kate. Tell the order in which the children were standing.

_____

_____

2. The school bus passes the park before it passes the bakery. It passes the swimming pool after it passes the bakery. The fire station is between the swimming pool and the bakery. In what order does the bus pass these places?

_____

_____

3. The principal's office is next to the entrance to the school. The third-grade room is closer to the office than the fifth-grade room is. A drinking fountain is between the third-grade room and the fifth-grade room. Tell what you would pass as you walked in the door and down the hall.

_____

_____

4. At the track meet, Dirk came in first. Bob came in after Dirk. Sarita came in after Dirk but before Bob. Helen came in before Bob but after Sarita. Who won first place, second place, third place, and fourth place?

_____

_____

Use with text pages 38–39.

Comparing and Ordering Numbers

Which of the two numbers is greater? Ring it.

1. 42	**2.** 121	**3.** 579	**4.** 180	**5.** 791	**6.** 4,989
52	212	597	179	781	3,989
7. 443	**8.** 220	**9.** 6,022	**10.** 325	**11.** 623	**12.** 5,399
463	202	6,202	225	643	5,491

Write > or < in each ◯.

13. 19 ◯ 91   **14.** 808 ◯ 708   **15.** 397 ◯ 479

16. 45 ◯ 54   **17.** 720 ◯ 730   **18.** 7,415 ◯ 6,415

19. 981 ◯ 979   **20.** 921 ◯ 912   **21.** 2,047 ◯ 2,147

22. 4,035 ◯ 4,050   **23.** 225 ◯ 223   **24.** 6,370 ◯ 6,307

25. 3,630 ◯ 3,629   **26.** 29 ◯ 49   **27.** 389 ◯ 383

28. List three numbers from least to greatest. 245, 175, 222

29. List three numbers from greatest to least. 87, 64, 92, 71

_____

Name _____

Ordinal Numbers

Al's house Ti's house Jo's house Luz's house Sam's house Sue's house Tom's house Ann's house Dom's house Lou's house

Use the picture to answer the questions.

1. Al lives in the first house.
Who lives in the eighth?

_____

2. Which house does Jo live in?

_____

3. Two people's names start with S.
Which houses do they live in?

_____ and _____

4. A dog lives in the fourth house.
Whose house is it?

_____

5. Which house does Ti live in?

_____

6. Tom walks from the tree to his
house. How many houses does
he walk by?

_____

7. Two people's name start with L.
Which houses do they live in?

_____ and _____

8. There are 21 houses on the
street. Steve lives in the next to
last house. What is his place on
the street?

_____

Rounding to the Nearest Ten

Ring the nearest ten for each number.

1. 32 → 30 or 40   **2.** 46 → 40 or 50   **3.** 63 → 60 or 70

4. 25 → 20 or 30   **5.** 79 → 70 or 80   **6.** 14 → 10 or 20

7. 87 → 80 or 90   **8.** 55 → 50 or 60   **9.** 68 → 60 or 70

10. 52 → 50 or 60   **11.** 39 → 30 or 40   **12.** 24 → 20 or 30

13. 16 → 10 or 20   **14.** 76 → 70 or 80   **15.** 45 → 40 or 50

Round to the nearest ten.

16. 52 → ___   **17.** 45 → ___   **18.** 92 → ___   **19.** 13 → ___

20. 69 → ___   **21.** 33 → ___   **22.** 37 → ___   **23.** 85 → ___

24. 19 → ___   **25.** 26 → ___   **26.** 11 → ___   **27.** 87 → ___

28. 73 → ___   **29.** 58 → ___   **30.** 74 → ___   **31.** 22 → ___

32. 94 → ___   **33.** 66 → ___   **34.** 28 → ___   **35.** 47 → ___

36. 44 → ___   **37.** 79 → ___   **38.** 93 → ___   **39.** 38 → ___

More About Rounding

Ring the nearest hundred or dollar.

1. 439 → 400 or 500   **2.** 722 → 700 or 800   **3.** 693 → 600 or 700

4. 825 → 800 or 900   **5.** 574 → 500 or 600   **6.** 361 → 300 or 400

7. $5.62 → $5.00 or $6.00   **8.** $3.69 → $3.00 or $4.00

9. $7.35 → $7.00 or $8.00   **10.** $8.13 → $8.00 or $9.00

Round to the nearest hundred.

11. 272 → _____   **12.** 445 → _____   **13.** 917 → _____

14. 660 → _____   **15.** 739 → _____   **16.** 708 → _____

17. 550 → _____   **18.** 334 → _____   **19.** 862 → _____

20. 911 → _____   **21.** 728 → _____   **22.** 284 → _____

Round to the nearest dollar.

23. $5.70 → _____   **24.** $4.77 → _____   **25.** $8.39 → _____

26. $1.52 → _____   **27.** $6.46 → _____   **28.** $3.29 → _____

29. $4.69 → _____   **30.** $2.99 → _____   **31.** $7.34 → _____

32. $2.89 → _____   **33.** $7.22 → _____   **34.** $6.75 → _____

35. $1.22 → _____   **36.** $5.50 → _____   **37.** $3.60 → _____

Name _____

Understanding the Question

Read each problem. Then underline the question
that asks the same thing.

1. Rob and Sam were in a talking
contest. Rob talked for 8 hours.
Sam talked for 11 hours. How
many more hours did Sam talk
than Rob?

    A How many hours did Rob
and Sam talk in all?

    B How many fewer hours did
Rob talk than Sam?

2. Lisa spent an afternoon watching
birds. In the first hour, she saw
34 birds. In the second hour, she
counted 17 birds. What was the
total number of birds Lisa saw?

    A How many birds did Lisa see
in all?

    B How many more birds did
Lisa see the first hour than
the second hour?

Write a question you can answer using either addition
or subtraction.

3. Evelyn and Roberto went rock
collecting. Evelyn found 7
sandstones. Roberto found 5
sandstones.

_____

_____

_____

_____

4. Alice and her father went
fishing. Alice caught 5 bass.
Her father caught 9 bass.

_____

_____

_____

_____

Reading and Writing 4-Digit Numbers

Tell how many thousands, hundreds, tens, and ones.
Then write the number.

1.

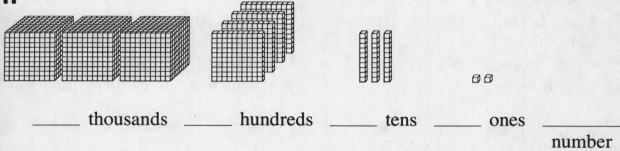

_____ thousands _____ hundreds _____ tens _____ ones _____
number

2.

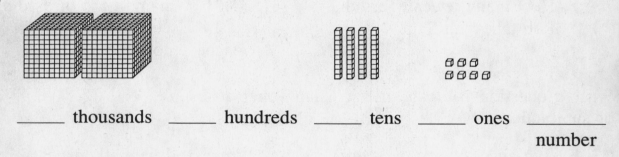

_____ thousands _____ hundreds _____ tens _____ ones _____
number

What is the value of the digit 4 in each of these
numbers? Write **4, 40, 400,** or **4,000.**

3. 2,143 _____

4. 1,241 _____

5. 3,482 _____

6. 4,631 _____

7. 8,314 _____

8. 2,490 _____

Write the numbers from the box that have the
given value.

9. greater than 4,300 _____

10. less than 2,500 _____

1,778	3,637
2,465	4,723

Understanding Thousands

Write the digit in the given place for 523,604.

1. thousands _____

2. hundreds _____

3. ones _____

4. ten thousands _____

5. tens _____

6. hundred thousands _____

Write the numbers from the box in
which the digit 6 has the given value.

7. 6,000 _____

8. 600 _____

9. 60,000 _____

10. 600,000 _____

604,281	356,514
161,878	241,650
436,149	613,792
848,633	260,357

Write the number. Use a comma to separate the
thousands period and the ones period.

11. forty thousand, seven hundred thirty seven

_____

12. six hundred twenty-three thousand, four hundred

_____

13. seven hundred two thousand, three

_____

Telling Time

Write each time as you would see it on a digital clock.

1.

_____

2.

_____

3.

_____

4.

_____

5.

_____

6.

_____

7.

_____

8.

_____

9.

_____

Write each time two different ways.

10.

_____

_____

11.

_____

_____

Name _____

Telling Time to the Minute

Write each time with a.m. or p.m.

1. Breakfast

_____

2. Violin lesson

_____

3. Library time

_____

4. Reading group

_____

5. Swimming lesson

_____

6. School ends

_____

7. Baseball game

_____

8. Math group

_____

9. Art class

_____

10. Recess

_____

11. Wake up

_____

12. Science group

_____

Time

Use mental math to tell the time.
Read each story problem. Then write the time.

1.

School ended at 3:00. Anne's music lesson was one hour later. What time was Anne's lesson?

_____

2.

The tour at the museum started at 10:00 and ended 45 minutes later. What time did the tour end?

_____

3.

The science lesson began at 11:00. It ended 30 minutes later. What time did the lesson end?

_____

4.

The movie started at 2:00. It ended 1 hour and 45 minutes later. What time did it end?

_____

5.

Rosa	2 hours
Daniel	1 hour 25 minutes

The swimming practice started at 1:00. The box shows how long each child swam. Write the time each child left.

Rosa _____

Daniel _____

6.

Susan	1 hour 30 minutes
Arthur	50 minutes

The party started at 4:00. The box above shows how long each child stayed. Write the time each child left.

Susan _____

Arthur _____

Reading a Calendar

JANUARY	FEBRUARY	MARCH	APRIL
S M T W T F S	S M T W T F S	S M T W T F S	S M T W T F S
1 2 3 4 5	1 2	1 2	1 2 3 4 5 6
6 7 8 9 10 11 12	3 4 5 6 7 8 9	3 4 5 6 7 8 9	7 8 9 10 11 12 13
13 14 15 16 17 18 19	10 11 12 13 14 15 16	10 11 12 13 14 15 16	14 15 16 17 18 19 20
20 21 22 23 24 25 26	17 18 19 20 21 22 23	17 18 19 20 21 22 23	21 22 23 24 25 26 27
27 28 29 30 31	24 25 26 27 28	24 25 26 27 28 29 30	28 29 30
		31	

MAY	JUNE	JULY	AUGUST
S M T W T F S	S M T W T F S	S M T W T F S	S M T W T F S
1 2 3 4	1	1 2 3 4 5 6	1 2 3
5 6 7 8 9 10 11	2 3 4 5 6 7 8	7 8 9 10 11 12 13	4 5 6 7 8 9 10
12 13 14 15 16 17 18	9 10 11 12 13 14 15	14 15 16 17 18 19 20	11 12 13 14 15 16 17
19 20 21 22 23 24 25	16 17 18 19 20 21 22	21 22 23 24 25 26 27	18 19 20 21 22 23 24
26 27 28 29 30 31	23 24 25 26 27 28 29	28 29 30 31	25 26 27 28 29 30 31
	30		

SEPTEMBER	OCTOBER	NOVEMBER	DECEMBER
S M T W T F S	S M T W T F S	S M T W T F S	S M T W T F S
1 2 3 4 5 6 7	1 2 3 4 5	1 2	1 2 3 4 5 6 7
8 9 10 11 12 13 14	6 7 8 9 10 11 12	3 4 5 6 7 8 9	8 9 10 11 12 13 14
15 16 17 18 19 20 21	13 14 15 16 17 18 19	10 11 12 13 14 15 16	15 16 17 18 19 20 21
22 23 24 25 26 27 28	20 21 22 23 24 25 26	17 18 19 20 21 22 23	22 23 24 25 26 27 28
29 30	27 28 29 30 31	24 25 26 27 28 29 30	29 30 31

Use the calendar to help you solve the problems.
January is the first month. The sixth month is June.

Write the name of the day of the week.

1. April 10 _____

2. October 8 _____

3. August 25 _____

4. December 12 _____

5. March 23 _____

6. July 22 _____

7. February 20 _____

8. September 13 _____

Write the date.

9. first Monday of the eighth month _____

10. last Sunday of the third month _____

Extra Data

Find the data you need. Solve each problem. Then write the extra data.

1. All 5 family members went shopping. They left their house at 2:00 and got back home at 4:20. How many hours did the family shop?

_____

_____

2. Erin's mother got to the airport at 6:00. The family lives 1 hour from the airport. The flight leaves at 7:15. How long did Erin's mother wait for the plane?

_____

_____

3. School began at 8:00. The first recess was 1 hour and 20 minutes after school started. The recess was 10 minutes long. What time was recess?

_____

_____

4. Oscar took the bus to the movie. The movie started at 3:00 and lasted 1 hour and 25 minutes. The bus costs $1. What time did the movie end?

_____

_____

5. The math lesson started at 9:00 and lasted 45 minutes. There are 10 students in the math group. What time did math end?

_____

_____

6. Tanya practices the trumpet 1 hour each day. She started at 4:00. Her lesson costs $10. What time did Tanya stop practicing?

_____

_____

Name _____

Making a Purchase

Give the value of each set of coins. Write the name and the price of the most expensive item you could buy at the bookstore with each amount.

1.

_____

_____

2.

_____

_____

3.

_____

_____

4.

_____

_____

5.

_____

_____

6.

_____

_____

Write these amounts in words.

7. $2.45 _____

8. $0.63 _____

Estimating Amounts of Money

Estimate each amount. Then list the items you could buy.

1.

_____

_____

2.

_____

_____

3.

_____

_____

4.

_____

_____

5.

_____

_____

6.

_____

_____

Name _____

Counting Change

Some students in Mr. Janson's class are buying
get-well cards for Tina. Count the change below.
Write the numbers the clerk would say.

1. Mandy handed the clerk 50¢.

35¢ _____ _____

2. Greg handed the clerk 75¢.

63¢ _____ _____ _____

3. Don handed the clerk 50¢.

43¢ _____ _____ _____

4. Maria handed the clerk $1.00.

79¢ _____ _____ _____

5. Doug handed the clerk 75¢.

59¢ _____ _____ _____

6. Ann handed the clerk $1.00.

93¢ _____ _____ _____

7. Joyce handed the clerk 75¢.

54¢ _____ _____ _____

8. Jim handed the clerk $1.00.

88¢ _____ _____ _____

Name _____

Make an Organized List

To solve some problems, you may need to make an
organized list using the data in the problem.
Read each problem. Then make a list of data to help
you solve the problem.

1. For the baseball game, Trish can
wear a blue T-shirt or a red
T-shirt. She has white shorts
and navy blue shorts. How many
different outfits can she choose?

Organized List

2. At the baseball game, Bill can
choose one food item and one
drink. The foods he can choose
from are popcorn, peanuts, or a
pretzel. For a drink Bill can have
either hot chocolate or orange
juice. How many different ways
can Bill choose a snack?

Organized List

3. Martha and her mother can
attend the baseball game on
Friday, Saturday, or Sunday.
The games start at 6:00 p.m.
They can also came an hour
early and watch batting practice
at 5:00 p.m. How many choices
of arrival time do Martha and
her mother have?

Organized List

Special Sums

Find the sums.

1. 20 + 50 = _____   **2.** 40 + 70 = _____

3. 70 + 30 = _____   **4.** 30 + 60 = _____

5. 90 + 20 = _____   **6.** 60 + 60 = _____

7. 10 + 40 = _____   **8.** 80 + 20 = _____

9. 50 + 70 = _____   **10.** 90 + 10 = _____

11. 40 + 50 = _____   **12.** 90 + 70 = _____

13. 80 + 80 = _____   **14.** 90 + 60 = _____

15. 30 + 80 = _____   **16.** 20 + 60 = _____

17. 30 + 70 = _____   **18.** 80 + 10 = _____

19. 900 + 300 = _____   **20.** 800 + 900 = _____

21. 600 + 800 = _____   **22.** 700 + 800 = _____

23. 200 + 700 = _____   **24.** 600 + 600 = _____

25. 400 + 300 = _____   **26.** 200 + 200 = _____

27. 800 + 300 = _____   **28.** 600 + 900 = _____

29. 500 + 400 = _____   **30.** 400 + 900 = _____

31. 100 + 800 = _____   **32.** 600 + 200 = _____

33. 300 + 500 = _____   **34.** 700 + 700 = _____

Name _____

Estimating Sums Using Rounding

Estimate by rounding to the nearest ten.

1. 32   30
+ 68 + 70

100

2. 79
+ 67

3. 56
+ 39

4. 81
+ 58

5. 17
+ 46

6. 21
+ 35

7. 73
+ 66

8. 14
+ 45

Estimate by rounding to the nearest hundred or dollar.

9.   340
+ 280

10.   625
+ 403

11.   889
+ 350

12.   919
+ 479

13.   161
+ 349

14.   550
+ 105

15. $5.69
+ 1.19

16. $6.49
+ 7.77

17. $5.25
+ 8.88

18. $4.98
+ 0.65

19. $3.49
+ 9.25

20. $2.50
+ 8.49

21. $5.82
+ 0.59

22. $6.23
+ 2.54

23. $5.42
+ 3.89

Trading 10 Ones for 1 Ten

Trade 10 ones for 1 ten until there are fewer than 10 ones. Record your results. Use blocks if you need help.

1.

Tens	Ones
	10

TRADE >

Tens	Ones
___	___

2.

Tens	Ones
2	11

TRADE >

Tens	Ones
___	___

3.

Tens	Ones
4	13

TRADE >

Tens	Ones
___	___

4.

Tens	Ones
1	10

TRADE >

Tens	Ones
___	___

5.

Tens	Ones
6	12

TRADE >

Tens	Ones
___	___

6.

Tens	Ones
	19

TRADE >

Tens	Ones
___	___

7.

Tens	Ones
5	11

TRADE >

Tens	Ones
___	___

8.

Tens	Ones
3	14

TRADE >

Tens	Ones
___	___

9. 22 ones

Tens	Ones

10. 16 ones

Tens	Ones

11. 11 ones

Tens	Ones

12. 27 ones

Tens	Ones

13. 19 ones

Tens	Ones

14. 30 ones

Tens	Ones

Adding 2-Digit Numbers: Making the Connection

Use place value blocks to add the numbers.
Record what you did.

1. Add 17 and 29.

2. Add 22 and 23.

3. Add 34 and 57.

4. Add 19 and 26.

5. Add 12 and 39.

6. Add 16 and 24.

7. Add 11 and 37.

8. Add 42 and 16.

Use place value blocks to find two numbers
that add to 75. **Answers will vary. Possible answers shown.**

9. ◯ + ◯ = 75 **10.** ◯ + ◯ = 75 **11.** ◯ + ◯ = 75

12. ◯ + ◯ = 75 **13.** ◯ + ◯ = 75 **14.** ◯ + ◯ = 75

Adding 2-Digit Numbers

Find the sums.

1. 34
    + 7

2. 15
    + 54

3. 47
    + 48

4. 47
    + 5

5. 39
    + 55

6. 38
    + 54

7. 60
    + 25

8. 72
    + 4

9. 66
    + 27

10. 28
    + 4

11. 22
    + 39

12. 36
    + 36

13. 25
    + 32

14. 39
    + 55

15. 28
    + 36

16. 46
    + 29

17. 27
    + 25

18. 78
    + 12

19. 78
    + 40

20. 26
    + 39

21. 85
    + 27

22. 44
    + 76

23. 57
    + 93

24. 48
    + 62

25. 31
    + 69

26. 64
    + 39

27. 45
    + 83

28. 89
    + 56

29. 29
    + 19

30. 74
    + 28

31. 45 + 77

  45
+ 77

 122

32. 87 + 92

  87
+ 92

 179

33. 94 + 86

  94
+ 86

 180

34. 49 + 18

  49
+ 18

  67

35. 75 + 33

  74
+ 33

 107

36. 63 + 82

  63
+ 82

 145

37. 63 + 58

  63
+ 58

 121

38. 59 + 75

  59
+ 75

 134

Name _____

Guess and Check

Guess your answer. Then check.

1. The librarian made a display. The display included all the books that were about one of the animals with fur. It also included all the books that were about one of the birds. There were 29 books in the display. Which animal and which bird were the books about?

BOOKS AT THE LIBRARY	
Subject	How Many
Bears	17
Cats	27
Wolves	16
Eagles	8
Hawks	8
Owls	12
Snakes	19
Lizards	9

_____

2. Does the library have more books about cats and owls or about bears and hawks?

_____

3. The children in Mr. Flynn's class borrowed 21 books. They borrowed all the books about one reptile and all the books about one bird. Which reptile and which bird were the books about?

_____

4. Nine children want to write reports on reptiles. Each child needs to use 3 books. Are there enough books?

_____

5. Jim needs 4 books about bears. If 8 books about bears are out of the library, are enough left for Jim?

_____

6. Which subject has the most books: furry animals, birds, or reptiles?

_____

7. How many more books does the library have about wolves than about eagles?

_____

Name _____

Adding 3-Digit Numbers: One Trade

Find the Sums.

| 1. | 224
+ 930 | 2. | 28
+ 343 | 3. | 653
+ 175 | 4. | 318
+ 246 | 5. | 696
+ 282 |

| 6. | 524
+ 243 | 7. | 425
+ 862 | 8. | 290
+ 199 | 9. | 644
+ 644 | 10. | 513
+ 77 |

| 11. | 962
+ 537 | 12. | 279
+ 513 | 13. | 287
+ 471 | 14. | 697
+ 141 | 15. | 429
+ 239 |

| 16. | 38
+ 148 | 17. | 500
+ 500 | 18. | 672
+ 72 | 19. | 564
+ 252 | 20. | 668
+ 123 |

| 21. | 679
+ 180 | 22. | 345
+ 812 | 23. | 123
+ 321 | 24. | 564
+ 273 | 25. | 804
+ 691 |

26. 425 + 25   **27.** 708 + 481   **28.** 269 + 421   **29.** 810 + 609

Name _____

Adding 3-Digit Numbers

Find the Sums.

1. 655 + 847	**2.** 547 + 377	**3.** 316 + 462	**4.** 175 + 258	**5.** 675 + 59
6. 795 + 409	**7.** 236 + 467	**8.** 34 + 989	**9.** 907 + 794	**10.** 856 + 132
11. 578 + 839	**12.** 424 + 626	**13.** 544 + 885	**14.** 418 + 974	**15.** 857 + 743
16. 367 + 408	**17.** 276 + 854	**18.** 963 + 163	**19.** 196 + 365	**20.** 678 + 145
21. 459 + 795	**22.** 686 + 582	**23.** 642 + 558	**24.** 948 + 690	**25.** 867 + 595

26. 494 + 426   **27.** 954 + 388   **28.** 62 + 158   **29.** 748 + 197

Breaking Apart Numbers

Find the sums.

1. $14 + 6 =$ _____ **2.** $18 + 3 =$ _____ **3.** $12 + 4 =$ _____

4. $13 + 9 =$ _____ **5.** $15 + 5 =$ _____ **6.** $19 + 8 =$ _____

7. $16 + 8 =$ _____ **8.** $17 + 2 =$ _____ **9.** $14 + 4 =$ _____

10. $18 + 2 =$ _____ **11.** $12 + 9 =$ _____ **12.** $13 + 2 =$ _____

13. $15 + 8 =$ _____ **14.** $11 + 7 =$ _____ **15.** $14 + 3 =$ _____

16. $17 + 5 =$ _____ **17.** $16 + 7 =$ _____ **18.** $11 + 9 =$ _____

19. $\begin{array}{r} 1 \\ 9 \\ +9 \\ \hline \end{array}$	**20.** $\begin{array}{r} 7 \\ 9 \\ +8 \\ \hline \end{array}$	**21.** $\begin{array}{r} 5 \\ 8 \\ +8 \\ \hline \end{array}$	**22.** $\begin{array}{r} 9 \\ 2 \\ +9 \\ \hline \end{array}$	**23.** $\begin{array}{r} 4 \\ 8 \\ +6 \\ \hline \end{array}$	**24.** $\begin{array}{r} 5 \\ 9 \\ +8 \\ \hline \end{array}$
25. $\begin{array}{r} 8 \\ 6 \\ +7 \\ \hline \end{array}$	**26.** $\begin{array}{r} 7 \\ 3 \\ +5 \\ \hline \end{array}$	**27.** $\begin{array}{r} 4 \\ 9 \\ +6 \\ \hline \end{array}$	**28.** $\begin{array}{r} 5 \\ 5 \\ +5 \\ \hline \end{array}$	**29.** $\begin{array}{r} 6 \\ 5 \\ +8 \\ \hline \end{array}$	**30.** $\begin{array}{r} 9 \\ 8 \\ +6 \\ \hline \end{array}$
31. $\begin{array}{r} 1 \\ 5 \\ +8 \\ \hline \end{array}$	**32.** $\begin{array}{r} 3 \\ 9 \\ +5 \\ \hline \end{array}$	**33.** $\begin{array}{r} 3 \\ 8 \\ +7 \\ \hline \end{array}$	**34.** $\begin{array}{r} 9 \\ 3 \\ +8 \\ \hline \end{array}$	**35.** $\begin{array}{r} 2 \\ 7 \\ +6 \\ \hline \end{array}$	**36.** $\begin{array}{r} 4 \\ 6 \\ +3 \\ \hline \end{array}$

Column Addition

Find the sums.

1.
```
   45
   37
+  14
```
2.
```
   28
    7
+  34
```
3.
```
   70
   62
+  57
```
4.
```
   81
   29
+  45
```
5.
```
   11
   43
+  44
```

6.
```
   275
   563
+   50
```
7.
```
 $4.75
  4.28
+ 3.19
```
8.
```
   354
   295
+  877
```
9.
```
   675
   436
+  277
```
10.
```
  $1.54
   7.20
+  4.66
```

11.
```
   212
   489
+  312
```
12.
```
 $3.54
  0.17
+ 1.22
```
13.
```
   432
   109
+  281
```
14.
```
   345
   432
+  723
```
15.
```
 $0.62
  3.23
+ 7.41
```

16.
```
   528
   382
   650
+  135
```
17.
```
    46
   453
   328
+  342
```
18.
```
   285
   343
    79
+  62
```
19.
```
   189
   475
   682
+  137
```
20.
```
   755
   312
   419
+  107
```

21. $25 + 48 + 46$

22. $14 + 99 + 63 + 29$

Name _____

Adding 4-Digit Numbers

Two railroad companies are laying track across the country.
Each day they lay a different number of cross ties.
Find out the total number of cross ties finished by both
companies each day.

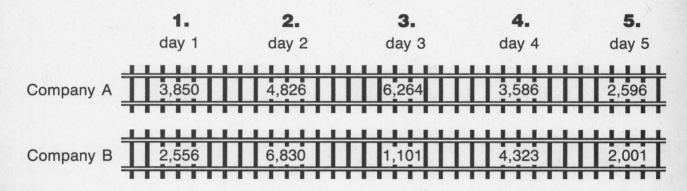

	1. day 1	**2.** day 2	**3.** day 3	**4.** day 4	**5.** day 5
Company A	3,850	4,826	6,264	3,586	2,596
Company B	2,556	6,830	1,101	4,323	2,001
Total	_____	_____	_____	_____	_____

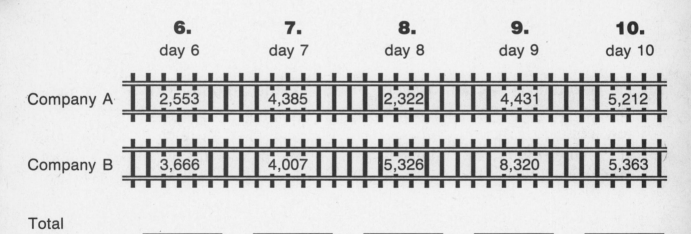

	6. day 6	**7.** day 7	**8.** day 8	**9.** day 9	**10.** day 10
Company A	2,553	4,385	2,322	4,431	5,212
Company B	3,666	4,007	5,326	8,320	5,363
Total	_____	_____	_____	_____	_____

Find the sums.

11. 4,628
      + 5,429

12. 3,109
      + 6,932

13. 5,336
      + 8,620

14. 4,421
      + 6,839

15. 4,212
      + 6,301

Deciding When to Estimate

Write **exact** if you need an exact answer. Write **estimate** if
an estimate will be enough to answer the question.

1. Paula's family is planning a trip. They plan to drive about 200 miles a day. Their trip will last 7 days. How far will they travel?

_____

2. Paula collects postcards. Big postcards are 50¢. Small postcards are 30¢. What will Paula pay for 1 large postcard and 3 small ones?

_____

3. Road maps cost 75¢. Paula has a $1 bill. How much change will she get if she buys a road map?

_____

4. Paula's father bought 80 gallons of gas during the trip. He paid about $1.25 a gallon at most places. About how much did he pay for gas for the trip?

_____

5. Paula counted 34 cows on her side of the highway. Her brother Ray counted 27 cows on his side. How many cows did they count in all?

_____

6. Paula's mother drives 40 miles an hour on the park roads. If she stops 2 times to let Ray take pictures with his camera, about how far will they go in 3 hours?

_____

7. Paula's lunch cost $1.86. Ray's lunch cost $2.35. How much did both lunches cost?

_____

8. Paula has $2.38 in her pocket. Ray has $1.85. Will they have enough to buy a deck of cards for $3.00?

_____

Using Data from a Catalog

Use the table. Solve.

```
GOOD VALUE CAMPING EQUIPMENT
2-Person Tent        $89.50      Air Mattress          $3.00
4-Person Tent        $139.00     Foam Sleeping Pad     $9.00
Good Sleeping Bag    $39.75      Best Sleeping Bag     $69.00
Flashlight           $2.75       Lantern               $15.00
```

1. Which will cost more, one 4-person tent or two 2-person tents?

_____

2. Brad has $10. How much change will he get if he buys an air mattress?

_____

3. What would it cost to buy a lantern and a good sleeping bag?

_____

4. How much will Diane save if she buys an air mattress instead of a foam sleeping pad?

_____

5. Maggie and a friend want to buy equipment for a camping trip. What items could they buy if they have only $145 to spend?

_____

6. Scot has $75. Does he have enough to buy the best sleeping bag and a foam sleeping pad?

_____

7. Batteries for the flashlight cost $2. How much will the flashlight and batteries cost together?

_____

8. How much would it cost to buy a good sleeping bag, an air mattress, and a 2-person tent?

_____

Name _____

Special Differences

Find the differences.

1. 80 − 50   **2.** 120 − 60   **3.** 900 − 500   **4.** 1,200 − 400

_____   _____   _____   _____

5. 130 − 60   **6.** 1,100 − 600   **7.** 150 − 70   **8.** 80 − 30

_____   _____   _____   _____

9. 1,400 − 900 **10.** 600 − 70   **11.** 1,000 − 400 **12.** 1,300 − 500

_____   _____   _____   _____

13. 120 − 30   **14.** 180 − 90   **15.** 140 − 80   **16.** 3,000 − 500

_____   _____   _____   _____

17. Subtract 300 from 500.   **18.** Subtract 80 from 150.

_____   _____

19. Subtract 90 from 120.   **20.** Subtract 400 from 1,100.

_____   _____

21. Find the difference between   **22.** Find the difference between
1,000 and 700.   1,200 and 900.

_____   _____

23. What is 1,400 minus 800?   **24.** What is 700 minus 500?

_____   _____

Estimating Differences Using Rounding

Estimate by rounding to the nearest ten.

1. 38
− 12

2. 54
− 26

3. 81
− 37

4. 85
− 52

5. 26
− 22

6. 42
− 28

Estimate by rounding to the nearest hundred or dollar.

7. 489
− 108

8. 635
− 287

9. 946
− 533

10. 803
− 675

11. 378
− 279

12. 539
− 150

13. $6.50
− 3.19

14. $4.69
− 2.55

15. $7.09
− 6.49

16. $8.40
− 2.78

17. $5.50
− 0.63

18. $6.27
− 4.61

Round to the nearest dollar and solve.

19. About how much less than $4.00 is $1.50?

20. About how much more than $2.20 is $6.00?

_____

_____

Trading 1 Ten for 10 Ones

Trade 1 ten for 10 ones.

1.

Tens	Ones
6	4

TRADE ⟩

Tens	Ones
5	14
6̸	4̸

2.

Tens	Ones
5	3

TRADE ⟩

Tens	Ones
5	3

3.

Tens	Ones
1	2

TRADE ⟩

Tens	Ones
1	2

4.

Tens	Ones
7	8

TRADE ⟩

Tens	Ones
7	8

5.

3	18
4̸	8̸

6. 2 9 **7.** 5 0 **8.** 9 3 **9.** 1 8

10. 8 6 **11.** 3 1 **12.** 7 2 **13.** 2 4 **14.** 4 0

15. 6 7 **16.** 3 8 **17.** 1 1 **18.** 5 5 **19.** 6 7

20. 8 9 **21.** 2 3 **22.** 5 8 **23.** 7 4 **24.** 9 1

Subtracting 2-Digit Numbers: Making the Connection

1. With play money, use 3 dimes and
2 pennies to show 32¢.
Take away 17¢.
You must trade 1 dime for 10 pennies.
What is 32¢ minus 17¢?

_____

Use play money to practice subtraction with trading.

2. Subtract 12¢ from 41¢.

_____

3. Subtract 18¢ from 54¢.

_____

4. Subtract 14¢ from 22¢.

_____

5. Subtract 25¢ from 44¢.

_____

6. Subtract 11¢ from 30¢.

_____

7. Subtract 29¢ from 43¢.

_____

8. Allie had 45¢. She spent 29¢
for an apple. How much did
she have left?

_____

9. Noru had 67¢. He spent 49¢
for a pen. How much did he
have left?

_____

Circle the examples where you must trade to find the
answer. Do not solve.

| **10.** | 45
− 27 | **11.** | 91
− 11 | **12.** | 80
− 70 | **13.** | 25
− 16 | **14.** | 61
− 14 |

Name _____

Subtracting 2-Digit Numbers

Find the differences.

1.	$\begin{array}{r}40\\-12\\\hline\end{array}$	**2.**	$\begin{array}{r}63\\-39\\\hline\end{array}$	**3.**	$\begin{array}{r}80\\-27\\\hline\end{array}$	**4.**	$\begin{array}{r}96\\-38\\\hline\end{array}$	**5.**	$\begin{array}{r}83\\-22\\\hline\end{array}$

6.	$\begin{array}{r}83\\-77\\\hline\end{array}$	**7.**	$\begin{array}{r}95\\-56\\\hline\end{array}$	**8.**	$\begin{array}{r}63\\-11\\\hline\end{array}$	**9.**	$\begin{array}{r}82\\-76\\\hline\end{array}$	**10.**	$\begin{array}{r}91\\-65\\\hline\end{array}$

11.	$\begin{array}{r}68\\-52\\\hline\end{array}$	**12.**	$\begin{array}{r}71\\-2\\\hline\end{array}$	**13.**	$\begin{array}{r}43\\-25\\\hline\end{array}$	**14.**	$\begin{array}{r}66\\-37\\\hline\end{array}$	**15.**	$\begin{array}{r}52\\-14\\\hline\end{array}$

16.	$\begin{array}{r}81\\-12\\\hline\end{array}$	**17.**	$\begin{array}{r}94\\-76\\\hline\end{array}$	**18.**	$\begin{array}{r}85\\-27\\\hline\end{array}$	**19.**	$\begin{array}{r}83\\-9\\\hline\end{array}$	**20.**	$\begin{array}{r}59\\-30\\\hline\end{array}$

21.	$\begin{array}{r}80\\-67\\\hline\end{array}$	**22.**	$\begin{array}{r}46\\-3\\\hline\end{array}$	**23.**	$\begin{array}{r}75\\-27\\\hline\end{array}$	**24.**	$\begin{array}{r}43\\-18\\\hline\end{array}$	**25.**	$\begin{array}{r}55\\-36\\\hline\end{array}$

26. $59 - 42$ **27.** $32 - 18$ **28.** $56 - 48$ **29.** $90 - 53$

30. $72 - 45$ **31.** $25 - 6$ **32.** $43 - 8$ **33.** $62 - 59$

Make a Table

Make a table to solve these problems.

1. When Carla practices her music lesson for 15 minutes, she gets a gold star. How many stars will she get if she practices for 60 minutes?

_____

Minutes of practice	15	30
Number of stars	1	2

2. Every day at camp, Eddie learns 4 new songs. How many new songs will he know after 5 days at camp?

_____

Days at camp	1	2	3
Number of songs	4	8	12

3. In the school band, Mark sets up 1 music stand for every 2 players. How many stands will he set up for 16 players?

_____

Number of players	2	4	6	8
Number of stands	1	2	3	4

4. When Dan practices his horn for 10 minutes, his teacher gives him two stickers. How long will he have to practice to get 12 stickers?

_____

Minutes of practice	10	20	30
Number of stars	2	4	6

5. Cherise listens to music while she does her paper route. While 1 song plays, she can deliver 5 papers. How many songs will she hear if she has 50 papers to deliver?

_____

Songs	1	2	3	4
Papers	5	10	15	20

6. Angie is selling tickets to a band concert. For every 5 tickets she sells, she gets 2 points. She needs 14 points for a stuffed animal. How many tickets must she sell?

_____

Tickets	5	10	15
Points	2	4	6

Subtracting 3-Digit Numbers: One Trade

Find the differences.

1. 732
     − 141

2. 244
     − 73

3. 817
     − 382

4. 753
     − 272

5. 671
     − 333

6. 819
     − 584

7. 135
     − 84

8. 781
     − 27

9. 980
     − 252

10. 734
      − 71

11. 438
      − 229

12. 644
      − 526

13. 249
      − 168

14. 384
      − 92

15. 848
      − 663

16. 776
      − 285

17. 641 − 450 _____

18. 338 − 153 _____

19. 162 − 48 _____

20. Subtract 258 from 871. _____

21. Subtract 374 from 982. _____

22. Find the difference
between 625 and 431. _____

23. How much less
than 474 is 81? _____

Subtracting 3-Digit Numbers

Find the differences.

1. $\begin{array}{r} 765 \\ -\ 376 \end{array}$	**2.** $\begin{array}{r} 814 \\ -\ 635 \end{array}$	**3.** $\begin{array}{r} 932 \\ -\ 894 \end{array}$	**4.** $\begin{array}{r} 843 \\ -\ 658 \end{array}$
5. $\begin{array}{r} 754 \\ -\ 559 \end{array}$	**6.** $\begin{array}{r} 829 \\ -\ 76 \end{array}$	**7.** $\begin{array}{r} 356 \\ -\ 277 \end{array}$	**8.** $\begin{array}{r} 777 \\ -\ 488 \end{array}$
9. $\begin{array}{r} 548 \\ -\ 269 \end{array}$	**10.** $\begin{array}{r} 695 \\ -\ 385 \end{array}$	**11.** $\begin{array}{r} 752 \\ -\ 548 \end{array}$	**12.** $\begin{array}{r} 764 \\ -\ 288 \end{array}$
13. $\begin{array}{r} 635 \\ -\ 308 \end{array}$	**14.** $\begin{array}{r} 566 \\ -\ 78 \end{array}$	**15.** $\begin{array}{r} 354 \\ -\ 268 \end{array}$	**16.** $\begin{array}{r} 915 \\ -\ 26 \end{array}$
17. $\begin{array}{r} 442 \\ -\ 384 \end{array}$	**18.** $\begin{array}{r} 456 \\ -\ 78 \end{array}$	**19.** $\begin{array}{r} 563 \\ -\ 274 \end{array}$	**20.** $\begin{array}{r} 744 \\ -\ 566 \end{array}$

21. $647 - 259$ **22.** $356 - 197$ **23.** $747 - 59$ **24.** $934 - 235$

25. $945 - 297$ **26.** $567 - 499$ **27.** $603 - 477$ **28.** $443 - 281$

Use with text pages 136–137.

Using Critical Thinking

Subtract. Check your answers.

1. Subtract   Check

$$\begin{array}{r} 863 \\ -\ 242 \\ \hline \end{array}$$
$$\begin{array}{r} 621 \\ +\ 242 \\ \hline \end{array}$$

2. Subtract   Check

$$\begin{array}{r} 738 \\ -\ 596 \\ \hline \end{array}$$
$$\begin{array}{r} 142 \\ +\ 596 \\ \hline \end{array}$$

3.
$$\begin{array}{r} 43 \\ -\ 25 \\ \hline \end{array}$$

4.
$$\begin{array}{r} 41 \\ -\ 8 \\ \hline \end{array}$$

5.
$$\begin{array}{r} 60 \\ -\ 26 \\ \hline \end{array}$$

6.
$$\begin{array}{r} 72 \\ -\ 36 \\ \hline \end{array}$$

7.
$$\begin{array}{r} 121 \\ -\ 39 \\ \hline \end{array}$$

8.
$$\begin{array}{r} 457 \\ -\ 189 \\ \hline \end{array}$$

9.
$$\begin{array}{r} 821 \\ -\ 445 \\ \hline \end{array}$$

10.
$$\begin{array}{r} 748 \\ -\ 59 \\ \hline \end{array}$$

11.
$$\begin{array}{r} 450 \\ -\ 166 \\ \hline \end{array}$$

12.
$$\begin{array}{r} 542 \\ -\ 308 \\ \hline \end{array}$$

13.
$$\begin{array}{r} 367 \\ -\ 348 \\ \hline \end{array}$$

14.
$$\begin{array}{r} 686 \\ -\ 299 \\ \hline \end{array}$$

15.
$$\begin{array}{r} 314 \\ -\ 106 \\ \hline \end{array}$$

16.
$$\begin{array}{r} 819 \\ -\ 279 \\ \hline \end{array}$$

17.
$$\begin{array}{r} 546 \\ -\ 187 \\ \hline \end{array}$$

Subtracting Across a Middle Zero

Find the differences.

1. 504
− 275

2. 805
− 386

3. 508
− 369

4. 308
− 267

5. 908
− 77

6. 706
− 380

7. 440
− 328

8. 206
− 142

9. 900
− 316

10. 305
− 185

11. 506
− 275

12. 700
− 248

13. 702
− 548

14. 908
− 79

15. 500
− 269

16. 304
− 199

17. 307
− 289

18. 706
− 259

19. 300
− 177

20. 843
− 56

21. 308 − 179　**22.** 467 − 69　**23.** 700 − 284　**24.** 207 − 159

25. 570 − 499　**26.** 450 − 267　**27.** 348 − 283　**28.** 656 − 67

Estimating Differences in Amounts of Money

Estimate each difference. Then find the exact
difference.

1. $2.45
       − 1.33

2. $8.21
       − 1.70

3. $8.34
       − 3.40

4. $6.00
       − 3.75

5. $9.60
       − 4.80

6. $2.37
       − 0.45

7. $9.83
       − 5.30

8. $8.40
       − 3.32

9. $9.00
       − 6.25

10. $6.21
        − 1.20

11. $12.40
        − 1.98

12. $6.38
        − 2.44

13. $5.47 − $3.40

14. $7.09 − $2.99

15. $1.24 − $1.13

16. How much is $650 minus $2.98?

17. Subtract $3.98 from $9.00.

Subtracting 4-Digit Numbers

Find the differences.

1.　4,374
　　− 2,256

2.　6,606
　　− 1,429

3.　5,295
　　− 2,883

4.　7,746
　　− 4,385

5.　5,843
　　− 3,561

6.　8,220
　　−　876

7.　3,173
　　−　652

8.　9,451
　　− 4,179

9.　3,682
　　− 1,340

10.　5,663
　　− 4,249

11.　6,202
　　− 1,956

12.　7,031
　　− 2,968

13. 6,170 − 388

14. 4,631 − 2,430

15. 2,846 − 1,593

16. 5,645 − 1,829

17. 7,059 − 5,343

18. 8,838 − 6,369

19.　$79.00
　　−　31.58

20.　$48.32
　　−　10.96

21.　$52.91
　　−　30.78

Choosing a Calculation Method

Choose a calculation method for each problem. Then solve.
Tell if you used mental math, paper and pencil, or a calculator.
Use each method at least twice.

1. Angela read 100 pages in one book and 35 pages in another. How many pages did she read in all?

2. Roy is mailing two letters. If each letter needs 59¢ in postage, what will it cost to mail the letters?

3. Toby bought a book for $2.95 and a magazine for $1.75. How much did he pay altogether?

4. Sue wanted to read 500 pages during her vacation. She read 1 book with 123 pages, 1 with 137 pages, and 1 with 129 pages. How many more pages must she read to reach her goal?

5. Art spent $12.99 for a new dictionary, $1.98 for a baseball story, and $1.53 for a fine at the library. How much did he spend in all?

6. Darrin is learning to use his word processor. After 1 week, he could type 23 words in one minute. After 2 weeks, he could type 33 words in one minute. How many more words per minute could he type after the second week than he could type after the first?

Multiple-Step Problems

Solve.

1. Frank had saved $18. He spent $10 on a baseball bat. Then he earned $5 mowing a lawn. He bought 2 birthday cards at $1 each. How much money did Frank have left?

_____

2. It cost Molly $0.79 for a packet of zinnia seeds. She spent $0.89 on a pack of pole bean seeds and $0.59 for marigold seeds. She gave the clerk $3. How much change did she get back?

_____

3. Mr. Wilson wanted to sell his car so he advertised it in the paper at $2.00 a day for 2 days. He spent another $9.46 in telephone calls. How much did he spend in all?

_____

4. Sally wanted to make a puppet. She spent $4.11 on felt, $0.39 on eyes, and $0.99 on yarn for hair. How much did it cost Sally to make a puppet?

_____

5. Ryan used 14 travel pictures for his report on Asia. 6 were of China and 5 were of Japan. The rest were of Korea. How many were of Korea?

_____

6. In the first week of June, 10 birds were born at the zoo. In the next week, 8 birds were born. 3 left to go to another zoo. How many were left?

_____

Reading Bar and Picture Graphs

1. The bar graph shows that a polar

bear weighs _____ kg and a

grizzly bear weighs _____ kg.
How much more does a polar
bear weigh?

_____

2. How much more does a brown
bear weigh than a black bear?

_____

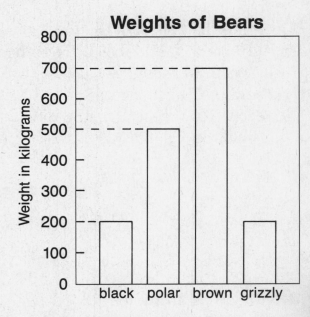

Weights of Bears

This picture graph shows the
number of books sold by a
bookstore last week.

Books Sold Last Week

3. How many books were sold on
Monday?

_____

4. On which day did the store sell
the fewest books?

_____

5. On which day did the store sell
the most books?

_____

6. How many books were sold on
Friday?

_____

Name _____

Collecting and Organizing Data

Mrs. Earle's class talked about how much money each student earned in one week for helping with chores at home.

Money Earned for Chores in 1 Week

Sarah	$2	Jessica	$3
Allison	$4	Blair	$4
Kesha	$4	Susan	$3
Justin	$2	Alice	$4
Don	$4	Daniel	$5
Brian	$3	Patrick	$2
Tanya	$2	Ken	$3
Arthur	$3	David	$3
Marsha	$5	Andrew	$3

1. Make a tally chart that shows the different amounts that students earned.

2. Look at your tally chart.
How many students earned $2? _____

3. How many students earned $4? _____

4. What amount was earned by the fewest students? _____

5. What amount was earned by the most students? _____

Making Bar Graphs

1. Scientists learn about birds by studying them carefully. The table below shows the weight of different birds. Complete the graph at the right to show the data on the table.

Weight of Birds in Grams	
Hummingbird	5
Cardinal	45
Flycatcher	15
Bunting	30

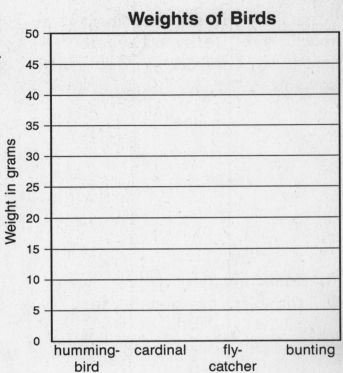

Weights of Birds

2. Make a list of 4 different subjects studied in the third grade. Have members of your class vote on their favorite. Record their votes. Then complete the graph. What will you name your graph?

Making Picture Graphs

1. Make a picture graph below to show the amount of items brought to a recycling center. Give your graph a title. The graph has been started for you.

Amounts at Recycling Center	
	Tons
Cans	2
Newspapers	10
Cardboard Boxes	7
Glass Bottles	5

Each 🥤 means _____ .

2. Choose 6 classmates. Have them tell you their favorite sport. Ask them to choose from tennis, baseball, and swimming. Make a picture graph to show your findings. What picture will you use?

Exploring Algebra

Find the number for each word. You may want to use a calculator.

A = 1	B = 2	C = 3
D = 4	E = 5	F = 6
G = 7	H = 8	I = 9
J = 10	K = 11	L = 12
M = 13	N = 14	O = 15
P = 16	Q = 17	R = 18
S = 19	T = 20	U = 21
V = 22	W = 23	X = 24
Y = 25	Z = 26	

1. algebra _____

2. addition _____

3. the _____

4. zoo _____

5. Write 2 words with a number less than 20.

_____

_____

6. Write 3 words with a number more than 20 but less than 40.

_____

7. Try to write a word that gives a total of exactly 40.

_____

8. Write the name of your school and the last name of your teacher. Then find the number for each word. Write the numbers. Which is greater?

_____

_____

Name _____

Look for a Pattern

Look for a pattern to help you solve the problems.

1. Donnie is making up a silly song with a lot of verses. The first time he sang it, it had 2 verses. The second time he sang it, it had 4 verses. The third time he sang it, it had 6 verses. How many verses will it have if he sings it 8 times?

_____

2. When she was 4 years old, Carol wrote a poem with 3 lines. When she was 5, she wrote a poem with 5 lines, and when she was 6, she wrote one with 9 lines. When she was 7, she wrote one with 15 lines. How many lines will be in a poem she writes when she is 8 years old?

_____

3. Frank is writing a book. The first week he wrote 5 pages. The second week he wrote 10 pages. The third week he wrote 15 pages. How many pages did he write the sixth week?

_____

4. Ruth made one sign for the writing club on the first day. The next day she made 3 signs. The third day she made 5 signs. How many signs did she make on the fifth day?

_____

5. Jolene likes to learn the meanings of new words. On Monday she learned 3 words. On Tuesday she learned 6 words. On Wednesday she learned 9 words. How many words did she learn on Friday?

_____

6. Lori had 30¢ to spend this week. On Sunday she spent no money. On Monday she spent 5¢. On Tuesday she spent 10¢. On Wednesday she spent 15¢. On what day was all her money gone?

_____

Name _____

Analyzing Data

The list shows data from a survey. Use the data to complete the exercises.

How many minutes of math homework is best?		
Students in Mr. C's Class	Students in Ms. R's Class	Students in Mrs. L's Class
30	10	30
20	30	30
10	30	20
10	20	20
20	10	10
10	30	20
30	30	10
10	30	20
10	30	30
10	30	10

1. Complete this table. Use the data above.

	10 minutes	_____	_____
Mr. C's class			
_____			
_____			

2. Draw a conclusion about how many minutes of math homework Mr. C's

class thinks is best compared to the other 2 classes? _____

_____

3. Draw a conclusion about how many minutes of math homework Mrs.

L's class thinks is best. _____

_____

4. Draw a conclusion about how many minutes of math homework Ms. R's class likes compared to the other 2 classes.

_____

Name _____

Probability: Fair and Unfair Games

Look at this game. Players drop counters
onto the game board. A player scores a point
each time a counter is completely inside the
space with his or her letter.

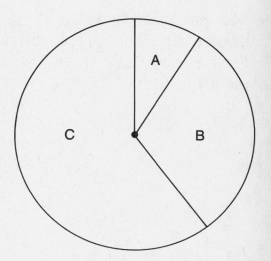

1. Is it a fair game? _____

2. Which player will probably

have the highest score? _____

3. Which player will probably

have the lowest score? _____

Write **fair** or **unfair** for each game board.

4.

5.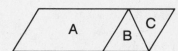

6.

_____ _____ _____

These are tallies for 2 different game boards. Are the games fair?
Write **fair** or **unfair**.

7.
A	⧸⧸⧸⧸ ⧸⧸⧸⧸ //
B	⧸⧸⧸⧸ ////
C	⧸⧸⧸⧸ ⧸⧸⧸⧸ /

8.
A	⧸⧸⧸⧸ ⧸⧸⧸⧸ ⧸⧸⧸⧸ /
B	⧸⧸⧸⧸ /
C	⧸⧸⧸⧸ ///

_____ _____

9. Study the game. Would you like to play
this game? Why or why not? Is one
player more likely to win than another?

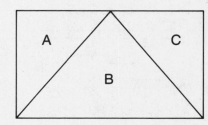

_____

_____

Making Predictions from Line Graphs

Megan has made a graph for each plant in her garden. Each graph shows how the plant grew in 3 weeks. Predict the height of each plant in the fourth week.

1.

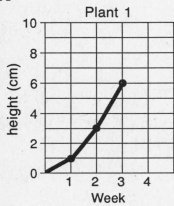

2.

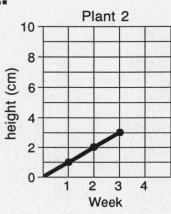

3.

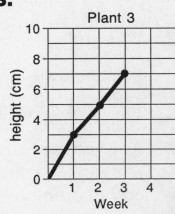

These graphs show the amount of time it takes for birds to eat birdseed from a feeder. Predict how many centimeters full each birdfeeder will be at Week 4.

4.

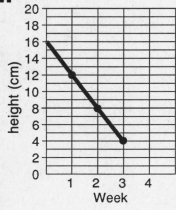

5.

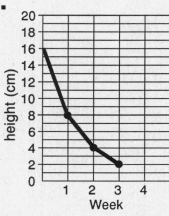

6.

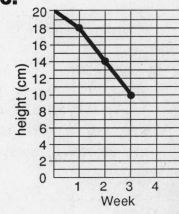

Using a Calculator

Use a calculator to solve the problems.

1. How many more points did Jerry West score than Bob Petit?

_____

BASKETBALL RECORDS		
Name	Games	Points
Wilt Chamberlain	1,045	31,419
Elgin Baylor	846	23,148
Jerry West	932	25,192
Bob Petit	792	20,880
Oscar Robertson	1,040	26,710

2. How many points did Oscar Robertson and Jerry West score altogether?

_____

3. How many more games did Wilt Chamberlain play than Elgin Baylor?

_____

4. How many points' difference is there between the highest and the lowest scorer on the table?

_____

5. How many more games did Jerry West play than Elgin Baylor?

_____

6. What is the total points scored by all five players?

_____

7. How many more games would Bob Petit have to play to reach 1,000 games?

_____

8. One year, Larry Bird tried 455 free throws. He made 414 of them. How many times did he miss?

_____

9. Donna practiced free throws at the playground. She tried 1,346 free throws one summer. She missed 217 times. How many did she make?

_____

Measuring Length in Inches

Estimate each object's length. Check your estimates by measuring to the nearest inch.

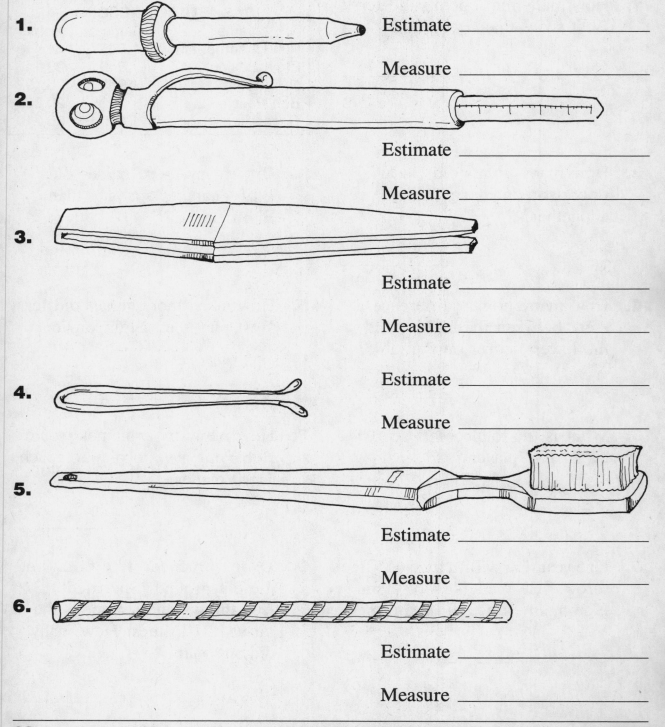

1. Estimate _____

   Measure _____

2. Estimate _____

   Measure _____

3. Estimate _____

   Measure _____

4. Estimate _____

   Measure _____

5. Estimate _____

   Measure _____

6. Estimate _____

   Measure _____

Estimating Length: Using a Benchmark

Measure the length of your foot.

Write the length. _____

Use your foot as a benchmark to estimate these
lengths. Check your estimates by measuring.
Compare your answers to a partner's
answer. Explain why they are different.

_____

1. Width of your classroom door

estimate: _____

measure: _____

2. Width of your desk

estimate: _____

measure: _____

3. Length of a baseball bat

estimate: _____

measure: _____

4. Your partner's height (Hint:
have your partner lie down.)

estimate: _____

measure: _____

5. Width of your chair

estimate: _____

measure: _____

6. Width of the hall outside your
classroom

estimate: _____

measure: _____

7. Length of your pencil

estimate: _____

measure: _____

8. Length of your book bag

estimate: _____

measure: _____

Foot, Yard, and Mile

Ring the better estimate.

1. How high is a grown tree?

   A 30 miles   **B** 30 feet

2. How long is a football field?

   A 100 yards   **B** 100 miles

3. How far can a boy walk in 1 hour?

   A 3 yards   **B** 3 miles

4. How high is a ceiling?

   A 3 feet   **B** 3 yards

5. How tall is a stop sign?

   A 8 feet   **B** 8 yards

6. How wide is a street?

   A 10 miles   **B** 10 yards

7. How long is a bed?

   A 2 feet   **B** 2 yards

8. How long is a bus?

   A 15 yards   **B** 15 miles

9. The height of a chair

   A less than 1 foot

   B more than 1 foot

10. An hour car ride

   A less than 1 mile

   B more than 1 mile

11. The height of a building

   A less than 1 yard

   B more than 1 yard

12. The height of a man

   A less than 1 yard

   B more than 1 yard

Name _____

Perimeter

Use a calculator to find the perimeter of each figure.

1.

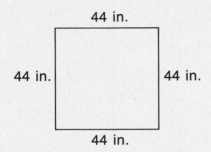

44 in.

44 in.   44 in.

44 in.

_____

2.

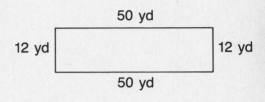

50 yd

12 yd   12 yd

50 yd

_____

3.

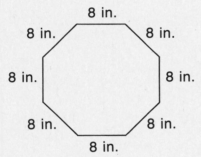

8 in.

8 in.   8 in.

8 in.   8 in.

8 in.   8 in.

8 in.

_____

4.

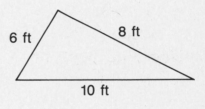

6 ft   8 ft

10 ft

_____

5. How many feet of fence are needed for the yard?

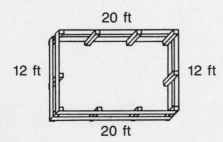

20 ft

12 ft   12 ft

20 ft

_____

6. How far is it around the picture frame?

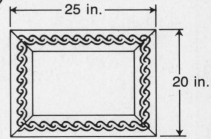

25 in.

20 in.

_____

Use Logical Reasoning

Use logical reasoning to solve each problem.

1. Pete asked Al how much money he had. Al said he had less than 80¢, but more than 75¢. He did not have an even number of cents. There was no 9 in the number. How much money did Al have?

_____

2. Henry asked Erin how many points her team scored in the softball game. "We scored an odd number of points," Erin said. "It was more than 4 and less than 9, and it was not 5." How many points did the team score?

_____

3. Mom asked Stacy how many boys and girls were in her class. Stacy said, "There is one more boy than girls. There are 21 students in all." How many boys and girls are in the class?

_____

4. "I have 5 coins," said Elton. "Only one is a quarter. They add up to 56¢." What coins could Elton have?

_____

5. Juanita and John are playing a number game. Juanita is thinking of a number between 1 and 100. John asks Juanita questions to guess the number. Juanita answers only yes or no.

Is it less than 50?	no
Is it an odd number?	yes
Is it more than 75?	yes
Does it end with 5?	yes
Is it 95?	no

What number is Juanita thinking of? _____

Deciding When to Estimate

Write whether to measure or estimate. Tell why.

1. Mrs. Sanchez is buying new curtains for her kitchen. Should she estimate or measure the size of the windows?

_____

2. Alex is putting the batter for muffins into 12 individual muffin tins. Should Alex measure or estimate the batter?

_____

3. Mr. Richards is cutting wallpaper to hang in his hall. Should he estimate or measure the length of wallpaper?

_____

4. Karen's grandfather is building an outdoor gym. Should he measure or estimate the length of boards he needs?

_____

5. You need rice to add to a recipe. Should you measure or estimate the amount?

_____

6. Perry is finishing a basket. Should he measure or estimate the length he needs to cut for a handle?

_____

7. You are shaping dough for dinner rolls. Should you estimate or measure each amount of dough?

_____

8. You want to buy a rug for your den. Should you estimate or measure the amount of floor space?

_____

9. Mrs. Carlson needs to wrap a present. Should she estimate or measure the amount of ribbon she needs?

_____

10. You need to add milk to a recipe to make a custard. Should you estimate or measure the amount of milk?

_____

Weight

> 9 pennies weigh about 1 ounce.
> 1 package of butter weighs about 1 pound.

Write **more** or **less** on the line to make each sentence true.

1. An apple weighs _____ than 1 ounce.

2. A dime weighs _____ than 1 ounce.

3. A math book weighs _____ than 1 ounce.

4. A crayon weighs _____ than 1 pound.

5. A cat weighs _____ than 1 pound.

6. An eraser weighs _____ than 1 pound.

7. A pencil weighs _____ than 1 pound.

8. A desk weighs _____ than 1 pound.

Choose the best estimate of weight.

9. Large book

2 oz or 2 lb

10. Hamburger

4 oz or 4 lb

Capacity and Temperature

1 quart = 4 cups	1 pint = 2 cups
1 quart = 2 pints	1 gallon = 4 quarts

Ring the better measure.

1. Coffee mug

A 1 cup   **B** 1 quart

2. Shampoo bottle

A 1 pint   **B** 1 gallon

Is this more than, less than, or the same as 1 pint?

3. 1 cup _____   **4.** 1 quart _____   **5.** 2 cups _____

Is this more than, less than, or the same as 1 quart?

6. 2 pints _____   **7.** 3 cups _____   **8.** 1 gallon _____

Is this more than, less than, or the same as 1 gallon?

9. 7 pints _____   **10.** 4 quarts _____   **11.** 5 quarts _____

The degree Fahrenheit (°F) is a unit for measuring temperature.

Write the reading for each thermometer.

12.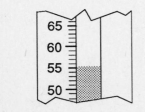

_____

13.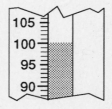

_____

Using Data from a Chart

The Raptor Center in Minnesota is a hospital for birds, such as bald eagles and red-tailed hawks. Here is a chart showing why these birds came to the Raptor Center in 1988. Use the chart to solve the problems.

	Bald Eagle	Red-Tailed Hawk
Shot	9	5
Trapped	5	3
Poisoned	5	0
Hurt	11	51
Other reasons	25	24

1. How many bald eagles came to the Raptor Center in 1988?

_____

2. Did more red-tailed hawks or bald eagles come to the Raptor Center in 1988?

_____

3. How many more birds came in because they were shot than because they were trapped?

_____

4. In which category did the largest number of bald eagles come to the Raptor Center: Shot, Trapped, Hurt, Poisoned, or Other reasons?

_____

5. In 1988, 31 of the bald eagles that came to the Raptor Center were too sick or hurt to be released. How many bald eagles got better and were released into the wild?

_____

6. How many birds came to the Raptor Center because they were trapped or poisoned?

_____

7. If 548 birds of all kinds came to the Raptor Center in 1988, how many birds were *not* bald eagles or red-tailed hawks?

_____

Name _____

Understanding Multiplication

Review the key actions and the operations you can use. Then read each problem. Tell which action it shows, write which operation you need to use, then solve the problem.

Key Action	Operation
Put together	Add
Take away Compare Find missing part	Subtract
Put together same- size sets	Multiply

1. Pam bought a book for $9 and a record for $3. How much did she spend?

_____

_____

2. Suzy earned $2 each day for 8 days. How much did she earn?

_____

_____

3. Len had $10. He spent $5 for a game. How much was left?

_____

_____

4. Mario had $23. He earned another $4 baby-sitting. How much does he have now?

_____

_____

5. Don bought 6 mugs. Each mug cost $2. What was the total cost?

_____

_____

6. Rick earned $6 each morning he worked. He worked for 3 mornings. How much did Rick earn?

_____

_____

Name _____

More About Multiplication

In Japan, farmers use straw baskets to hold eggs.
Each basket holds 5 eggs.

Fill in the chart with the total number of eggs
for each number of baskets.

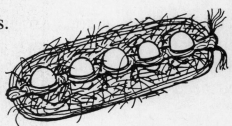

	1. 1 basket	2. 2 baskets	3. 3 baskets	4. 4 baskets	5. 5 baskets
number of eggs	5				

Write how many.

6.

$$\begin{array}{r} 2 \\ 2 \\ +\ 2 \\ \hline \end{array}$$

$3 \times 2 =$ _____

7.

$$\begin{array}{r} 4 \\ 4 \\ +\ 4 \\ \hline \end{array}$$

$3 \times 4 =$ _____

8.

$$\begin{array}{r} 6 \\ 6 \\ 6 \\ +\ 6 \\ \hline \end{array}$$

$4 \times 6 =$ _____

9.

$$\begin{array}{r} 4 \\ 4 \\ 4 \\ 4 \\ +\ 4 \\ \hline \end{array}$$

$5 \times 4 =$ _____

Name _____

A Factor of 2

Multiply.

1. $\begin{array}{r} 2 \\ \times 2 \\ \hline \end{array}$ **2.** $\begin{array}{r} 2 \\ \times 9 \\ \hline \end{array}$ **3.** $\begin{array}{r} 5 \\ \times 2 \\ \hline \end{array}$ **4.** $\begin{array}{r} 8 \\ \times 2 \\ \hline \end{array}$ **5.** $\begin{array}{r} 2 \\ \times 3 \\ \hline \end{array}$

6. $\begin{array}{r} 9 \\ \times 2 \\ \hline \end{array}$ **7.** $\begin{array}{r} 4 \\ \times 2 \\ \hline \end{array}$ **8.** $\begin{array}{r} 2 \\ \times 2 \\ \hline \end{array}$ **9.** $\begin{array}{r} 7 \\ \times 2 \\ \hline \end{array}$ **10.** $\begin{array}{r} 2 \\ \times 6 \\ \hline \end{array}$

11. $\begin{array}{r} 2 \\ \times 5 \\ \hline \end{array}$ **12.** $\begin{array}{r} 2 \\ \times 9 \\ \hline \end{array}$ **13.** $\begin{array}{r} 8 \\ \times 2 \\ \hline \end{array}$ **14.** $\begin{array}{r} 2 \\ \times 6 \\ \hline \end{array}$ **15.** $\begin{array}{r} 4 \\ \times 2 \\ \hline \end{array}$

16. $\begin{array}{r} 3 \\ \times 2 \\ \hline \end{array}$ **17.** $\begin{array}{r} 2 \\ \times 8 \\ \hline \end{array}$ **18.** $\begin{array}{r} 2 \\ \times 2 \\ \hline \end{array}$ **19.** $\begin{array}{r} 9 \\ \times 2 \\ \hline \end{array}$ **20.** $\begin{array}{r} 5 \\ \times 2 \\ \hline \end{array}$

21. $\begin{array}{r} 8 \\ \times 2 \\ \hline \end{array}$ **22.** $\begin{array}{r} 7 \\ \times 2 \\ \hline \end{array}$ **23.** $\begin{array}{r} 2 \\ \times 3 \\ \hline \end{array}$ **24.** $\begin{array}{r} 2 \\ \times 6 \\ \hline \end{array}$ **25.** $\begin{array}{r} 2 \\ \times 5 \\ \hline \end{array}$

26. $\begin{array}{r} 2 \\ \times 9 \\ \hline \end{array}$ **27.** $\begin{array}{r} 4 \\ \times 2 \\ \hline \end{array}$ **28.** $\begin{array}{r} 6 \\ \times 2 \\ \hline \end{array}$ **29.** $\begin{array}{r} 3 \\ \times 2 \\ \hline \end{array}$ **30.** $\begin{array}{r} 2 \\ \times 8 \\ \hline \end{array}$

31. $2 \times 2 =$ _____ **32.** $2 \times 5 =$ _____ **33.** $2 \times 9 =$ _____

34. $2 \times 6 =$ _____ **35.** $3 \times 2 =$ _____ **36.** $7 \times 2 =$ _____

Name _____

A Factor of 5

Multiply.

1. $\begin{array}{r} 5 \\ \times\, 4 \\ \hline \end{array}$ **2.** $\begin{array}{r} 9 \\ \times\, 5 \\ \hline \end{array}$ **3.** $\begin{array}{r} 2 \\ \times\, 5 \\ \hline \end{array}$ **4.** $\begin{array}{r} 2 \\ \times\, 9 \\ \hline \end{array}$ **5.** $\begin{array}{r} 5 \\ \times\, 5 \\ \hline \end{array}$ **6.** $\begin{array}{r} 6 \\ \times\, 5 \\ \hline \end{array}$

7. $\begin{array}{r} 5 \\ \times\, 3 \\ \hline \end{array}$ **8.** $\begin{array}{r} 8 \\ \times\, 5 \\ \hline \end{array}$ **9.** $\begin{array}{r} 8 \\ \times\, 2 \\ \hline \end{array}$ **10.** $\begin{array}{r} 5 \\ \times\, 2 \\ \hline \end{array}$ **11.** $\begin{array}{r} 4 \\ \times\, 5 \\ \hline \end{array}$ **12.** $\begin{array}{r} 3 \\ \times\, 5 \\ \hline \end{array}$

13. $\begin{array}{r} 7 \\ \times\, 5 \\ \hline \end{array}$ **14.** $\begin{array}{r} 5 \\ \times\, 1 \\ \hline \end{array}$ **15.** $\begin{array}{r} 5 \\ \times\, 9 \\ \hline \end{array}$ **16.** $\begin{array}{r} 5 \\ \times\, 6 \\ \hline \end{array}$ **17.** $\begin{array}{r} 6 \\ \times\, 2 \\ \hline \end{array}$ **18.** $\begin{array}{r} 5 \\ \times\, 7 \\ \hline \end{array}$

19. $\begin{array}{r} 4 \\ \times\, 2 \\ \hline \end{array}$ **20.** $\begin{array}{r} 5 \\ \times\, 8 \\ \hline \end{array}$ **21.** $\begin{array}{r} 2 \\ \times\, 8 \\ \hline \end{array}$ **22.** $\begin{array}{r} 3 \\ \times\, 2 \\ \hline \end{array}$ **23.** $\begin{array}{r} 2 \\ \times\, 4 \\ \hline \end{array}$ **24.** $\begin{array}{r} 9 \\ \times\, 5 \\ \hline \end{array}$

25. $\begin{array}{r} 1 \\ \times\, 5 \\ \hline \end{array}$ **26.** $\begin{array}{r} 9 \\ \times\, 2 \\ \hline \end{array}$ **27.** $\begin{array}{r} 2 \\ \times\, 2 \\ \hline \end{array}$ **28.** $\begin{array}{r} 2 \\ \times\, 3 \\ \hline \end{array}$ **29.** $\begin{array}{r} 2 \\ \times\, 5 \\ \hline \end{array}$ **30.** $\begin{array}{r} 2 \\ \times\, 7 \\ \hline \end{array}$

31. $5 \times 4 =$ _____   **32.** $7 \times 5 =$ _____   **33.** $5 \times 6 =$ _____

34. $5 \times 5 =$ _____   **35.** $5 \times 2 =$ _____   **36.** $9 \times 5 =$ _____

37. $6 \times 5 =$ _____   **38.** $8 \times 5 =$ _____   **39.** $5 \times 3 =$ _____

40. $5 \times 7 =$ _____   **41.** $2 \times 5 =$ _____   **42.** $5 \times 8 =$ _____

43. $2 \times 6 =$ _____   **44.** $7 \times 2 =$ _____   **45.** $9 \times 2 =$ _____

A Factor of 9

Multiply.

1. 9
  × 3

2. 4
  × 2

3. 4
  × 9

4. 5
  × 3

5. 9
  × 6

6. 5
  × 8

7. 9
  × 9

8. 2
  × 5

9. 9
  × 7

10. 6
  × 2

11. 1
  × 2

12. 2
  × 7

13. 9
  × 5

14. 4
  × 5

15. 2
  × 9

16. 1
  × 9

17. 5
  × 7

18. 9
  × 8

19. 5
  × 1

20. 2
  × 6

21. 0
  × 5

22. 3
  × 9

23. 2
  × 2

24. 5
  × 4

25. 9
  × 0

26. 2
  × 8

27. 9
  × 4

28. 6
  × 5

29. 8
  × 2

30. 5
  × 9

31. $9 \times 6 =$ _____

32. $7 \times 2 =$ _____

33. $9 \times 4 =$ _____

34. $7 \times 5 =$ _____

35. $5 \times 9 =$ _____

36. $2 \times 3 =$ _____

37. $8 \times 9 =$ _____

38. $4 \times 2 =$ _____

39. $7 \times 9 =$ _____

Using Critical Thinking

Finish this fact list for the 2 facts.

$2 \times 1 =$ _____ $2 \times 4 =$ _____ $2 \times 7 =$ _____

$2 \times 2 =$ _____ $2 \times 5 =$ _____ $2 \times 8 =$ _____

$2 \times 3 =$ _____ $2 \times 6 =$ _____ $2 \times 9 =$ _____

Each product on the 2 fact list is _____ more than the one before. The

product of 2×10 must be _____ because _____.

Finish this fact list for the 5 facts.

$5 \times 1 =$ _____ $5 \times 4 =$ _____ $5 \times 7 =$ _____

$5 \times 2 =$ _____ $5 \times 5 =$ _____ $5 \times 8 =$ _____

$5 \times 3 =$ _____ $5 \times 6 =$ _____ $5 \times 9 =$ _____

Each product on the 5 fact list is _____ more than the one before. The

product of 5×10 must be _____ because _____.

Finish this fact list for the 9 facts.

$9 \times 1 =$ _____ $9 \times 4 =$ _____ $9 \times 7 =$ _____

$9 \times 2 =$ _____ $9 \times 5 =$ _____ $9 \times 8 =$ _____

$9 \times 3 =$ _____ $9 \times 6 =$ _____ $9 \times 9 =$ _____

Each product on the 9 fact list is _____ more than the one before. The product

of 9×10 must be _____ because _____.

Work Backward

Work backward to solve each problem.
You may want to use a calculator.

1. On Arbor Day, workers planted 10 trees at city hall. They left 2 on the truck because there was no room for them. They planted 4 others at the library. How many trees were on the truck when the workers started?

_____

2. For Veterans Day, the school decided to fly some flags. They bought 5 more flags to add to the ones they already had. They borrowed 4 others. Of the borrowed flags, 2 were torn and could not be used. The school flew 10 flags. How many flags did the school have to start with?

_____

3. To celebrate Presidents' Day, Mrs. Arden bought her family some apples. 3 were rotten and had to be thrown away. Mrs. Arden bought 4 more apples. Then she had 10 apples. How many apples did she buy the first time?

_____

4. On Independence Day the children went to a carnival. They bought a bag of balloons. 3 popped. 5 had holes in them. They had 20 balloons left. How many balloons were in the bag when they bought it?

_____

0 and 1 as Factors

Multiply.

1. $\begin{array}{r} 1 \\ \times\,1 \\ \hline \end{array}$
2. $\begin{array}{r} 0 \\ \times\,0 \\ \hline \end{array}$
3. $\begin{array}{r} 0 \\ \times\,1 \\ \hline \end{array}$
4. $\begin{array}{r} 2 \\ \times\,9 \\ \hline \end{array}$
5. $\begin{array}{r} 0 \\ \times\,5 \\ \hline \end{array}$

6. $\begin{array}{r} 0 \\ \times\,7 \\ \hline \end{array}$
7. $\begin{array}{r} 1 \\ \times\,9 \\ \hline \end{array}$
8. $\begin{array}{r} 3 \\ \times\,5 \\ \hline \end{array}$
9. $\begin{array}{r} 0 \\ \times\,2 \\ \hline \end{array}$
10. $\begin{array}{r} 4 \\ \times\,9 \\ \hline \end{array}$

11. $\begin{array}{r} 5 \\ \times\,9 \\ \hline \end{array}$
12. $\begin{array}{r} 0 \\ \times\,3 \\ \hline \end{array}$
13. $\begin{array}{r} 1 \\ \times\,4 \\ \hline \end{array}$
14. $\begin{array}{r} 3 \\ \times\,2 \\ \hline \end{array}$
15. $\begin{array}{r} 1 \\ \times\,5 \\ \hline \end{array}$

16. $\begin{array}{r} 1 \\ \times\,0 \\ \hline \end{array}$
17. $\begin{array}{r} 1 \\ \times\,6 \\ \hline \end{array}$
18. $\begin{array}{r} 4 \\ \times\,9 \\ \hline \end{array}$
19. $\begin{array}{r} 0 \\ \times\,4 \\ \hline \end{array}$
20. $\begin{array}{r} 5 \\ \times\,8 \\ \hline \end{array}$

21. $\begin{array}{r} 5 \\ \times\,5 \\ \hline \end{array}$
22. $\begin{array}{r} 0 \\ \times\,6 \\ \hline \end{array}$
23. $\begin{array}{r} 1 \\ \times\,3 \\ \hline \end{array}$
24. $\begin{array}{r} 0 \\ \times\,0 \\ \hline \end{array}$
25. $\begin{array}{r} 5 \\ \times\,7 \\ \hline \end{array}$

26. $8 \times 1 =$ _____
27. $5 \times 0 =$ _____
28. $9 \times 1 =$ _____

29. $9 \times 0 =$ _____
30. $7 \times 0 =$ _____
31. $0 \times 0 =$ _____

32. $1 \times 1 =$ _____
33. $6 \times 1 =$ _____
34. $4 \times 1 =$ _____

Use with text pages 226–227.

Mastering the Facts

Give these products as quickly as you can. Use what
you know about patterns to help you.

1. $\begin{array}{r} 1 \\ \times\, 0 \\ \hline \end{array}$ **2.** $\begin{array}{r} 5 \\ \times\, 4 \\ \hline \end{array}$ **3.** $\begin{array}{r} 6 \\ \times\, 1 \\ \hline \end{array}$ **4.** $\begin{array}{r} 6 \\ \times\, 5 \\ \hline \end{array}$ **5.** $\begin{array}{r} 1 \\ \times\, 7 \\ \hline \end{array}$

6. $\begin{array}{r} 2 \\ \times\, 6 \\ \hline \end{array}$ **7.** $\begin{array}{r} 0 \\ \times\, 7 \\ \hline \end{array}$ **8.** $\begin{array}{r} 1 \\ \times\, 2 \\ \hline \end{array}$ **9.** $\begin{array}{r} 5 \\ \times\, 6 \\ \hline \end{array}$ **10.** $\begin{array}{r} 9 \\ \times\, 5 \\ \hline \end{array}$

11. $\begin{array}{r} 1 \\ \times\, 5 \\ \hline \end{array}$ **12.** $\begin{array}{r} 1 \\ \times\, 6 \\ \hline \end{array}$ **13.** $\begin{array}{r} 1 \\ \times\, 3 \\ \hline \end{array}$ **14.** $\begin{array}{r} 0 \\ \times\, 3 \\ \hline \end{array}$ **15.** $\begin{array}{r} 7 \\ \times\, 5 \\ \hline \end{array}$

16. $2 \times 1 =$ _____   **17.** $1 \times 1 =$ _____   **18.** $0 \times 2 =$ _____

19. $9 \times 3 =$ _____   **20.** $3 \times 9 =$ _____   **21.** $0 \times 8 =$ _____

22. $1 \times 4 =$ _____   **23.** $0 \times 4 =$ _____   **24.** $3 \times 5 =$ _____

25. Find the product of 3 and 0. _____

26. What is 3 multiplied by 9? _____

27. Multiply 3 by 2. _____

28. What is the product of 5 and 7? _____

29. What is 9 multiplied by 8? _____

30. Multiply 9 by 9. _____

A Factor of 3

Multiply.

1. $\begin{array}{r} 3 \\ \times 3 \\ \hline \end{array}$
2. $\begin{array}{r} 6 \\ \times 3 \\ \hline \end{array}$
3. $\begin{array}{r} 3 \\ \times 7 \\ \hline \end{array}$
4. $\begin{array}{r} 2 \\ \times 5 \\ \hline \end{array}$
5. $\begin{array}{r} 3 \\ \times 9 \\ \hline \end{array}$

6. $\begin{array}{r} 2 \\ \times 7 \\ \hline \end{array}$
7. $\begin{array}{r} 3 \\ \times 3 \\ \hline \end{array}$
8. $\begin{array}{r} 2 \\ \times 3 \\ \hline \end{array}$
9. $\begin{array}{r} 2 \\ \times 6 \\ \hline \end{array}$
10. $\begin{array}{r} 8 \\ \times 3 \\ \hline \end{array}$

11. $\begin{array}{r} 3 \\ \times 8 \\ \hline \end{array}$
12. $\begin{array}{r} 9 \\ \times 3 \\ \hline \end{array}$
13. $\begin{array}{r} 3 \\ \times 4 \\ \hline \end{array}$
14. $\begin{array}{r} 2 \\ \times 3 \\ \hline \end{array}$
15. $\begin{array}{r} 5 \\ \times 3 \\ \hline \end{array}$

16. $\begin{array}{r} 2 \\ \times 4 \\ \hline \end{array}$
17. $\begin{array}{r} 3 \\ \times 2 \\ \hline \end{array}$
18. $\begin{array}{r} 8 \\ \times 3 \\ \hline \end{array}$
19. $\begin{array}{r} 3 \\ \times 3 \\ \hline \end{array}$
20. $\begin{array}{r} 3 \\ \times 9 \\ \hline \end{array}$

21. $\begin{array}{r} 2 \\ \times 8 \\ \hline \end{array}$
22. $\begin{array}{r} 5 \\ \times 3 \\ \hline \end{array}$
23. $\begin{array}{r} 3 \\ \times 4 \\ \hline \end{array}$
24. $\begin{array}{r} 2 \\ \times 9 \\ \hline \end{array}$
25. $\begin{array}{r} 3 \\ \times 7 \\ \hline \end{array}$

26. $3 \times 6 =$ _____
27. $3 \times 2 =$ _____
28. $4 \times 3 =$ _____

29. $7 \times 3 =$ _____
30. $3 \times 3 =$ _____
31. $3 \times 5 =$ _____

32. $3 \times 8 =$ _____
33. $7 \times 2 =$ _____
34. $9 \times 3 =$ _____

Use with text pages 238–239.

Finding Larger Doubles

Find the sums using mental math. Write
answers only.

1. $12 + 12 =$ ____   **2.** $9 + 9 =$ _____   **3.** $14 + 14 =$ ____

4. $15 + 15 =$ ____   **5.** $8 + 8 =$ _____   **6.** $6 + 6 =$ _____

7. $17 + 17 =$ ____   **8.** $11 + 11 =$ ____   **9.** $7 + 7 =$ _____

10. $16 + 16 =$ ____   **11.** $19 + 19 =$ ____   **12.** $10 + 10 =$ ____

Ring the letter of the sum that will help you find
the double.

13. $14 + 14$ **A** $20 + 4$ **B** $20 + 8$

14. $17 + 17$ **A** $20 + 14$ **B** $20 + 7$

15. $11 + 11$ **A** $10 + 1$ **B** $20 + 2$

16. $15 + 15$ **A** $20 + 10$ **B** $20 + 5$

17. $12 + 12$ **A** $20 + 2$ **B** $20 + 4$

18. $18 + 18$ **A** $20 + 16$ **B** $20 + 8$

Find the products.

19. $\begin{array}{r} 7 \\ \times\,3 \\ \hline \end{array}$ **20.** $\begin{array}{r} 6 \\ \times\,5 \\ \hline \end{array}$ **21.** $\begin{array}{r} 9 \\ \times\,8 \\ \hline \end{array}$ **22.** $\begin{array}{r} 6 \\ \times\,2 \\ \hline \end{array}$ **23.** $\begin{array}{r} 5 \\ \times\,7 \\ \hline \end{array}$

24. $\begin{array}{r} 2 \\ \times\,4 \\ \hline \end{array}$ **25.** $\begin{array}{r} 2 \\ \times\,7 \\ \hline \end{array}$ **26.** $\begin{array}{r} 9 \\ \times\,9 \\ \hline \end{array}$ **27.** $\begin{array}{r} 6 \\ \times\,0 \\ \hline \end{array}$ **28.** $\begin{array}{r} 2 \\ \times\,9 \\ \hline \end{array}$

Name _____

A Factor of 4

Multiply.

1. $\begin{array}{r} 4 \\ \times\, 4 \\ \hline \end{array}$ **2.** $\begin{array}{r} 6 \\ \times\, 4 \\ \hline \end{array}$ **3.** $\begin{array}{r} 4 \\ \times\, 2 \\ \hline \end{array}$ **4.** $\begin{array}{r} 2 \\ \times\, 7 \\ \hline \end{array}$ **5.** $\begin{array}{r} 9 \\ \times\, 4 \\ \hline \end{array}$

6. $\begin{array}{r} 5 \\ \times\, 4 \\ \hline \end{array}$ **7.** $\begin{array}{r} 4 \\ \times\, 6 \\ \hline \end{array}$ **8.** $\begin{array}{r} 2 \\ \times\, 4 \\ \hline \end{array}$ **9.** $\begin{array}{r} 4 \\ \times\, 3 \\ \hline \end{array}$ **10.** $\begin{array}{r} 8 \\ \times\, 4 \\ \hline \end{array}$

11. $\begin{array}{r} 3 \\ \times\, 8 \\ \hline \end{array}$ **12.** $\begin{array}{r} 2 \\ \times\, 4 \\ \hline \end{array}$ **13.** $\begin{array}{r} 2 \\ \times\, 5 \\ \hline \end{array}$ **14.** $\begin{array}{r} 4 \\ \times\, 9 \\ \hline \end{array}$ **15.** $\begin{array}{r} 7 \\ \times\, 4 \\ \hline \end{array}$

16. $\begin{array}{r} 3 \\ \times\, 2 \\ \hline \end{array}$ **17.** $\begin{array}{r} 6 \\ \times\, 4 \\ \hline \end{array}$ **18.** $\begin{array}{r} 4 \\ \times\, 9 \\ \hline \end{array}$ **19.** $\begin{array}{r} 3 \\ \times\, 4 \\ \hline \end{array}$ **20.** $\begin{array}{r} 4 \\ \times\, 2 \\ \hline \end{array}$

21. $\begin{array}{r} 8 \\ \times\, 4 \\ \hline \end{array}$ **22.** $\begin{array}{r} 3 \\ \times\, 9 \\ \hline \end{array}$ **23.** $\begin{array}{r} 4 \\ \times\, 6 \\ \hline \end{array}$ **24.** $\begin{array}{r} 2 \\ \times\, 6 \\ \hline \end{array}$ **25.** $\begin{array}{r} 3 \\ \times\, 3 \\ \hline \end{array}$

26. $4 \times 3 =$ _____   **27.** $6 \times 3 =$ _____   **28.** $4 \times 2 =$ _____

29. $4 \times 4 =$ _____   **30.** $4 \times 7 =$ _____   **31.** $9 \times 4 =$ _____

32. $5 \times 4 =$ _____   **33.** $6 \times 4 =$ _____   **34.** $4 \times 8 =$ _____

Name _____

Basic Facts That Are Squares

Find the products.

1. 8
   × 8

2. 4
   × 9

3. 9
   × 0

4. 8
   × 0

5. 5
   × 1

6. 4
   × 4

7. 7
   × 5

8. 2
   × 2

9. 6
   × 3

10. 8
    × 5

11. 0
    × 0

12. 3
    × 6

13. 6
    × 6

14. 3
    × 8

15. 4
    × 5

16. 9
    × 9

17. 9
    × 2

18. 6
    × 4

19. 7
    × 3

20. 5
    × 9

21. 1
    × 1

22. 9
    × 5

23. 4
    × 6

24. 6
    × 5

25. 4
    × 1

26. 5
    × 7

27. 8
    × 4

28. 1
    × 9

29. 7
    × 8

30. 5
    × 5

31. 3
    × 9

32. 3
    × 3

33. 2
    × 5

34. 8
    × 9

35. 7
    × 4

36. 6
    × 6

37. 5 × 3 = _____

38. 2 × 2 = _____

39. 4 × 9 = _____

40. 9 × 7 = _____

41. 5 × 9 = _____

42. 5 × 5 = _____

43. 4 × 4 = _____

44. 6 × 5 = _____

45. 7 × 7 = _____

Multiple-Step Problems

Solve.

1. Greg bought 2 packages of pencils for $1.39 each and 3 pens for $1.49 each. How much did he spend?

_____

2. Markers cost $1.29 each. Pens cost 2 for $1.99. Which would cost more, 2 pens or 2 markers? How much more?

_____

3. A package of paper has 500 sheets. If 9 children each take 8 sheets of paper, how many will be left in the package?

_____

4. Adele got 8 crayons for her eighth birthday, 16 crayons for her ninth birthday, and 32 crayons for her tenth birthday. At this rate, how many crayons will she get when she is 11?

_____

5. A package of computer paper costs $8.97. Disks for the computer cost $1.57 each. How much will Yuki spend for 1 package of paper and 2 disks?

_____

6. Bart has $25.00. If he buys a notebook for $3.49, paper for $1.98, and a pen for $2.49, how much will he have left?

_____

7. In Mark's class, 5 children have boxes with 8 crayons and 9 children have boxes with 16 crayons. How many crayons do they have altogether?

_____

8. Pens cost $0.89 each. About how many pens can Katie buy if she has $3.12?

_____

The Last Three Facts: 6 × 7, 6 × 8, 7 × 8

Find the products.

1. 9
   × 4

2. 9
   × 6

3. 8
   × 3

4. 8
   × 9

5. 8
   × 6

6. 0
   × 9

7. 7
   × 7

8. 8
   × 2

9. 8
   × 8

10. 4
    × 8

11. 7
    × 6

12. 5
    × 4

13. 9
    × 7

14. 5
    × 9

15. 2
    × 8

16. 8
    × 4

17. 3
    × 8

18. 9
    × 5

19. 1
    × 8

20. 3
    × 6

21. 9
    × 8

22. 9
    × 9

23. 6
    × 6

24. 3
    × 9

25. 3
    × 5

26. 8
    × 5

27. 9
    × 3

28. 4
    × 9

29. 7
    × 9

30. 9
    × 2

31. 5
    × 8

32. 8
    × 4

33. 3
    × 3

34. 5
    × 5

35. 8
    × 7

36. 9
    × 6

37. $7 \times 8 =$ _____

38. $6 \times 8 =$ _____

39. $6 \times 5 =$ _____

40. $2 \times 7 =$ _____

41. $4 \times 4 =$ _____

42. $2 \times 9 =$ _____

43. $5 \times 9 =$ _____

44. $8 \times 9 =$ _____

45. $6 \times 9 =$ _____

Missing Factors

Write the missing factor problems.

1. Paula said, "I know that $3 \times 4 = 12$. I can write two missing factor problems using that fact." What two problems can Paula write?

_____

2. Kyle said, "I know that $5 \times 6 = 30$. I can write two missing factor problems using that fact." What two problems can Kyle write?

_____

Find the missing factors.

3. $\boxed{} \times 5 = 10$ **4.** $4 \times \boxed{} = 20$ **5.** $\boxed{} \times 7 = 35$

6. $6 \times \boxed{} = 30$ **7.** $\boxed{} \times 2 = 16$ **8.** $3 \times \boxed{} = 24$

9. $7 \times \boxed{} = 28$ **10.** $\boxed{} \times 7 = 14$ **11.** $4 \times \boxed{} = 24$

12. $\boxed{} \times 3 = 21$ **13.** $8 \times \boxed{} = 32$ **14.** $\boxed{} \times 9 = 18$

Name _____

Mastering the Facts

Find the products. Practice giving the products
as quickly as possible.

1. $\begin{array}{r} 2 \\ \times 5 \\ \hline \end{array}$ **2.** $\begin{array}{r} 9 \\ \times 9 \\ \hline \end{array}$ **3.** $\begin{array}{r} 8 \\ \times 7 \\ \hline \end{array}$ **4.** $\begin{array}{r} 9 \\ \times 2 \\ \hline \end{array}$ **5.** $\begin{array}{r} 8 \\ \times 5 \\ \hline \end{array}$ **6.** $\begin{array}{r} 6 \\ \times 5 \\ \hline \end{array}$

7. $\begin{array}{r} 8 \\ \times 1 \\ \hline \end{array}$ **8.** $\begin{array}{r} 7 \\ \times 5 \\ \hline \end{array}$ **9.** $\begin{array}{r} 8 \\ \times 3 \\ \hline \end{array}$ **10.** $\begin{array}{r} 5 \\ \times 5 \\ \hline \end{array}$ **11.** $\begin{array}{r} 9 \\ \times 4 \\ \hline \end{array}$ **12.** $\begin{array}{r} 6 \\ \times 8 \\ \hline \end{array}$

13. $\begin{array}{r} 6 \\ \times 6 \\ \hline \end{array}$ **14.** $\begin{array}{r} 4 \\ \times 8 \\ \hline \end{array}$ **15.** $\begin{array}{r} 4 \\ \times 6 \\ \hline \end{array}$ **16.** $\begin{array}{r} 9 \\ \times 8 \\ \hline \end{array}$ **17.** $\begin{array}{r} 2 \\ \times 9 \\ \hline \end{array}$ **18.** $\begin{array}{r} 8 \\ \times 8 \\ \hline \end{array}$

19. $\begin{array}{r} 4 \\ \times 9 \\ \hline \end{array}$ **20.** $\begin{array}{r} 9 \\ \times 7 \\ \hline \end{array}$ **21.** $\begin{array}{r} 3 \\ \times 8 \\ \hline \end{array}$ **22.** $\begin{array}{r} 7 \\ \times 6 \\ \hline \end{array}$ **23.** $\begin{array}{r} 2 \\ \times 7 \\ \hline \end{array}$ **24.** $\begin{array}{r} 8 \\ \times 4 \\ \hline \end{array}$

25. $\begin{array}{r} 7 \\ \times 7 \\ \hline \end{array}$ **26.** $\begin{array}{r} 3 \\ \times 7 \\ \hline \end{array}$ **27.** $\begin{array}{r} 9 \\ \times 5 \\ \hline \end{array}$ **28.** $\begin{array}{r} 8 \\ \times 6 \\ \hline \end{array}$ **29.** $\begin{array}{r} 9 \\ \times 3 \\ \hline \end{array}$ **30.** $\begin{array}{r} 7 \\ \times 9 \\ \hline \end{array}$

31. $\begin{array}{r} 9 \\ \times 3 \\ \hline \end{array}$ **32.** $\begin{array}{r} 3 \\ \times 6 \\ \hline \end{array}$ **33.** $\begin{array}{r} 8 \\ \times 2 \\ \hline \end{array}$ **34.** $\begin{array}{r} 9 \\ \times 1 \\ \hline \end{array}$ **35.** $\begin{array}{r} 4 \\ \times 8 \\ \hline \end{array}$ **36.** $\begin{array}{r} 9 \\ \times 6 \\ \hline \end{array}$

37. $3 \times 9 =$ _____ **38.** $6 \times 8 =$ _____ **39.** $8 \times 9 =$ _____

Multiplying 3 Factors

Use mental math to find the products.
Use the groupings shown. Do the work in
parentheses first.

1. $2 \times (3 \times 4) =$ ___ **2.** $(2 \times 3) \times 4 =$ ___ **3.** $(2 \times 4) \times 3 =$ ___

4. $(3 \times 2) \times 1 =$ ___ **5.** $3 \times (2 \times 1) =$ ___ **6.** $(3 \times 1) \times 2 =$ ___

7. $(1 \times 1) \times 1 =$ ___ **8.** $2 \times (2 \times 2) =$ ___ **9.** $(3 \times 3) \times 3 =$ ___

Multiply. Use any groupings.

10. $4 \times 2 \times 3 =$ ___ **11.** $1 \times 6 \times 2 =$ ___ **12.** $2 \times 5 \times 4 =$ ___

13. $3 \times 2 \times 2 =$ ___ **14.** $4 \times 2 \times 5 =$ ___ **15.** $3 \times 3 \times 2 =$ ___

16. $6 \times 0 \times 7 =$ ___ **17.** $9 \times 1 \times 3 =$ ___ **18.** $8 \times 2 \times 1 =$ ___

19. $3 \times 4 \times 2 =$ ___ **20.** $4 \times 2 \times 4 =$ ___ **21.** $1 \times 1 \times 7 =$ ___

22. $2 \times 0 \times 9 =$ ___ **23.** $3 \times 1 \times 9 =$ ___ **24.** $8 \times 8 \times 0 =$ ___

25. $8 \times 7 \times 1 =$ ___ **26.** $3 \times 4 \times 3 =$ ___ **27.** $8 \times 2 \times 2 =$ ___

28. Find the product of 8 and 0 and 2. ___

29. Find the product of 2 and 5 and 3. ___

30. Find the product of 8 and 6 and 1. ___

Multiples

Complete the pyramid and its title. Give the
missing numbers.

1.

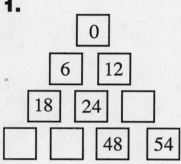

2.

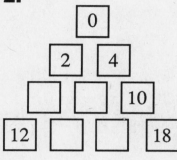

3.

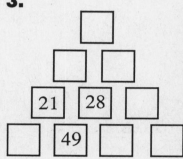

multiples of _____   _____   _____

4. These numbers are multiples of what number?

0, 3, 6, 12, 15, 18 _____

5. Find the first 5 multiples of 6. Use a calculator.

_____ _____ _____ _____ _____

6. Find the first 7 multiples of 8. Use a calculator.

_____ _____ _____ _____ _____ _____ _____

Find the products.

7. $\begin{array}{r} 3 \\ \times 7 \\ \hline \end{array}$	**8.** $\begin{array}{r} 9 \\ \times 7 \\ \hline \end{array}$	**9.** $\begin{array}{r} 6 \\ \times 6 \\ \hline \end{array}$	**10.** $\begin{array}{r} 9 \\ \times 0 \\ \hline \end{array}$	**11.** $\begin{array}{r} 4 \\ \times 8 \\ \hline \end{array}$
12. $\begin{array}{r} 7 \\ \times 5 \\ \hline \end{array}$	**13.** $\begin{array}{r} 6 \\ \times 7 \\ \hline \end{array}$	**14.** $\begin{array}{r} 9 \\ \times 4 \\ \hline \end{array}$	**15.** $\begin{array}{r} 8 \\ \times 8 \\ \hline \end{array}$	**16.** $\begin{array}{r} 7 \\ \times 8 \\ \hline \end{array}$

Name _____

Practicing the Facts

Find the products. Practice giving the products as quickly as possible.

1. 4 × 3

2. 3 × 6

3. 2 × 8

4. 2 × 2

5. 5 × 3

6. 1 × 7

7. 5 × 2

8. 0 × 0

9. 2 × 7

10. 5 × 4

11. 5 × 6

12. 8 × 3

13. 3 × 2

14. 9 × 3

15. 7 × 4

16. 4 × 4

17. 3 × 7

18. 3 × 5

19. 9 × 7

20. 7 × 7

21. 8 × 9

22. 5 × 8

23. 6 × 9

24. 7 × 6

25. 9 × 8

26. 6 × 7

27. 7 × 9

28. 8 × 8

29. 8 × 5

30. 4 × 9

31. 9 × 4 = _____

32. 7 × 5 = _____

33. 6 × 1 = _____

34. 6 × 6 = _____

35. 3 × 8 = _____

36. 4 × 5 = _____

37. Find the product of 7 and 6. _____

38. What is the product of 9 and 4? _____

Use with text pages 258–259. **PS-3**

Problems with More than One Answer

Choose a strategy that you know to solve each problem.

Some Strategies	
Act It Out	Use Objects
Choose an Operation	Draw a Picture
Make an Organized List	Guess and Check
Look for a Pattern	Make a Table
Use Logical Reasoning	Work Backward

1. There are 24 members in the school band. How many ways can they line up with the same number of people in each row?

_____

2. Angie's teacher asked the class to make groups with the same number of people in each group. If there are 30 children in the class, what size groups could they make?

_____

3. A checkerboard has 8 rows of squares with 8 squares in each row. How many squares are on a checkerboard?

_____

4. A chess player starts with 16 chess pieces. If 8 of them are pawns, how many are not pawns?

_____

5. Rudy and Kiesha are playing checkers. they each started with 12 checkers. Rudy lost 4 checkers and Kiesha lost 3. How many checkers are left on the board?

_____

6. Andrew and Uri played 54 games of chess. Andrew won 24 times. Uri won 17 times. How many times did nobody win?

_____

Space Figures

    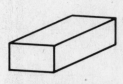

| sphere | cube | cylinder | cone | rectangular prism | pyramid |

Write **cube, sphere, cylinder, cone, rectangular prism,**
or **pyramid** for each object below.

1.

_____

2.

_____

3.

_____

4.

_____

5.

_____

6.

_____

7.

_____

8.

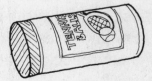

_____

Plane Figures

Write whether the picture or description reminds you of
a **square**, a **rectangle**, a **circle**, or a **triangle**.

1.

_____

2.

_____

3.

_____

4.

_____

5.

_____

6.

_____

7. 4 sides all the same length

_____

8. 3 sides and 3 corners

_____

Polygons and Segments

Write who made each shape.

1. A small square

_____

Andy's strips

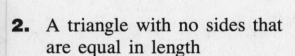

2. A triangle with no sides that
are equal in length

_____

Carlos's strips

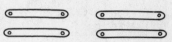

3. A rectangle

_____

Kathy's strips

4. A triangle with all sides that
are equal in length

_____

Nancy's strips

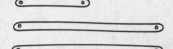

David's strips

5. A large square

_____

Sue Ellen's strips

6. A triangle with just two sides
that are equal in length

_____

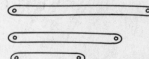

Polygons and Angles

Decide if the angle is a right angle, greater than a right angle, or less than a right angle.

1. _____

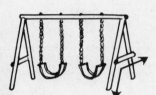

2. _____

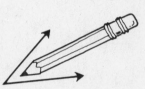

3. _____

4. _____

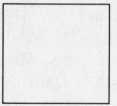

5. _____

6. _____

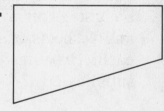

Put an **X** on all of the right angles in each figure.

7.

8.

9.

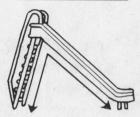

Write the number of segments and angles for each figure.

10.

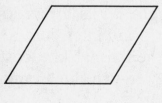

segments _____

angles _____

11.

segments _____

angles _____

12.

segments _____

angles _____

Determining Reasonable Answers

Use the list to decide whether the answer to each problem is reasonable or unreasonable. Explain.

Price List	
String	$0.98
Wood	$0.25 per piece
Paper	$0.12 per sheet

1. Maria made a kite. She bought 1 roll of string, 2 pieces of wood, and 3 sheets of paper. How much did her supplies cost? Answer: $3.00

_____

_____

2. Ming wanted to make 2 birds out of paper. Each bird took 2 sheets of paper. She gave the clerk $1.00. How much change did Ming get back? Answer: $0.52

_____

_____

Solve. Use any problem solving strategy.

3. Pablo decided to make a mobile out of string and paper. He bought 1 roll of string at $1.50 and 4 sheets of paper at $0.14 each. How much did his supplies cost?

_____

4. Perry, Megan, Trisha, and Daniel made sculptures from clay. Perry's was bigger than Daniel's. Trisha's was bigger than Daniel's but smaller than Perry's. Megan's was smaller than Daniel's. Whose sculpture was largest?

_____

5. The train for Boston leaves at 12:05 p.m. The bus to the train station from Esther's house takes 30 minutes. If Esther catches the 11:15 a.m. bus, how long will she wait for the train?

_____

6. Frank bought 3 kits for making kites. The 2 box kites cost $3.00 each and the animal kite cost $2.70. How much did Frank spend in all?

_____

Sorting Polygons

These polygons belong to different families.
Answer the riddles about the polygons and
their families. HINT: Some polygons belong
to more than one family.

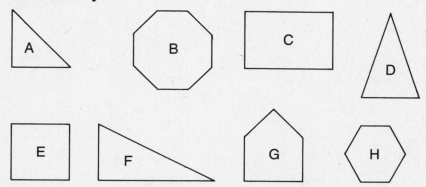

1. All the polygons in the Right family have right angles. Which polygons
are in the Right family?

_____

2. All the polygons in the Odd family have an odd number of sides.
Which polygons are in the Odd family?

_____

3. All the sides of the polygons in the Equal family are the same length.
Which polygons are in the Equal family?

_____

4. Ann Odd said, "My cousin Odd Odd is very strange. All of her sides
are different lengths. Which polygon is cousin Odd Odd?

_____

5. Which family has the most members, the Rights, the Odds, or the Equals?

_____

Symmetry

Draw lines of symmetry.
Trace and fold if you are not sure.

Draw 1 line of symmetry.

1.

2.

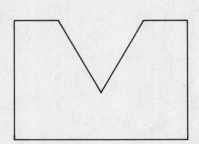

3.

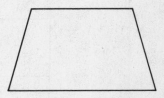

Draw 2 lines of symmetry.

4.

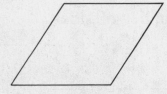

5.

6.

7.

8.

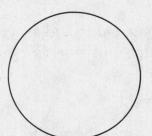

9.

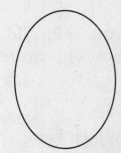

Congruence

Ring the figure that is congruent
to the first one in the row.

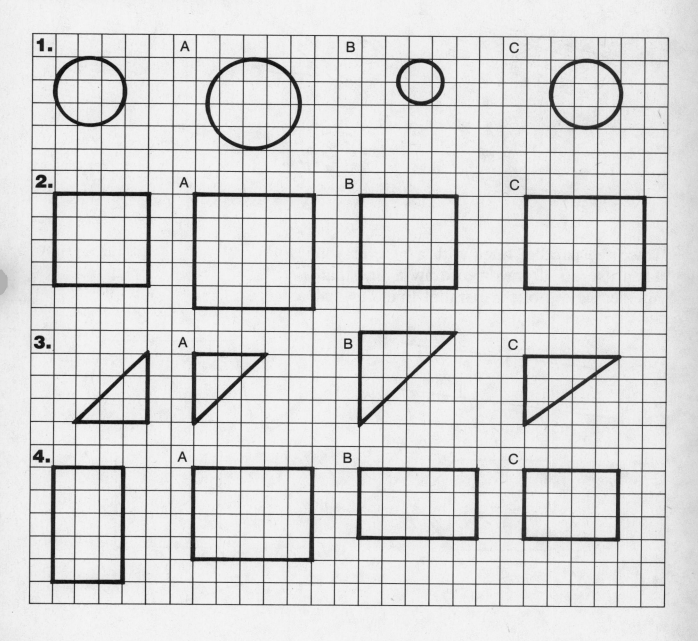

Parallel Lines

Ring the pictures that suggest parallel lines.

1.

2.

3.

4.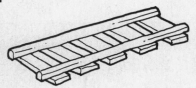

5.

6.

Trace the parallel lines with a blue crayon.
Then use a red crayon to draw a line that
intersects both of the parallel lines.

7.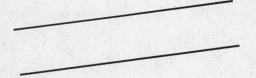

8.

9.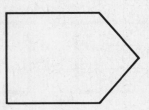

10.

11.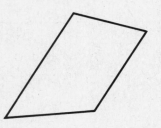

12.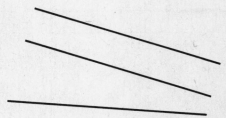

Name _____

Coordinate Geometry

Use the map to answer the questions.

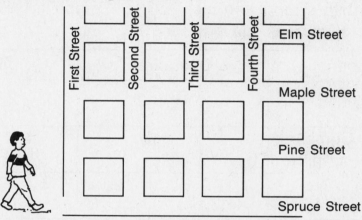

Martin always starts at the corner of First Street and Spruce Street.

1. If Martin goes right 2 blocks and up 3 blocks, he will be at the corner of what streets?

_____

2. If Martin goes up 2 blocks and right 3 blocks, he will be at the corner of what streets?

_____

3. The number pair (3,3) locates the corner of what streets?

_____

4. The number pair (1,1) locates the corner of what streets?

_____

5. Give a number pair to locate the corner of Third Street and Pine Street.

_____

6. Give a number pair to locate the corner of Second Street and Maple Street.

_____

7. Give a number pair to locate the corner of First Street and Elm Street.

_____

8. Give a number pair to locate the corner of Second Street and Spruce Street.

_____

Understanding Division

1. This table shows the key actions you have learned. It shows the operation used and the math symbol for each action. Complete the table by filling in the missing operations and symbols.

Action	Operation	Symbol
Put together	add	+
Take away; Compare; Find a missing part		
Put together same-size sets		
Share a set equally		

For each problem, write the action and operation used. Then write the answer.

2. A baby weighed 7 pounds at birth in March. In June, the baby weighed 11 pounds. How much more did it weigh in June than in March?

_____

_____

3. Mr. Martin changed 4 tires on each car. There were 3 cars. How many tires did he change in all?

_____

_____

4. A hiker saw 4 swans in the pond and 3 others sleeping near a nest. How many swans did the hiker see?

_____

_____

5. There were 6 hikers on a walk. Their leader brought 12 oranges for their snack. Each hiker got the same number of oranges. How many oranges did each hiker get?

_____

_____

Name _____

More About Division

Find the quotients. Use counters and cups if you need help.

1.

Share 8 equally 2 ways.

$$8 \div 2 = \underline{\qquad}$$

2.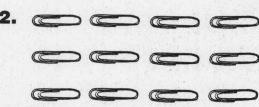

Share 12 equally 3 ways.

$$12 \div 3 = \underline{\qquad}$$

3.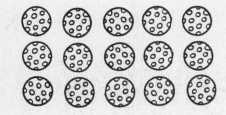

$$15 \div 3 = \underline{\qquad}$$

4.

$$14 \div 2 = \underline{\qquad}$$

5.

$$12 \div 2 = \underline{\qquad}$$

6.

$$6 \div 3 = \underline{\qquad}$$

7.

$$15 \div 5 = \underline{\qquad}$$

8.

$$8 \div 4 = \underline{\qquad}$$

Name _____

Dividing by 2 and 3

Divide.

1. $14 \div 2 =$ _____   **2.** $3 \div 3 =$ _____   **3.** $10 \div 2 =$ _____

4. $12 \div 3 =$ _____   **5.** $12 \div 2 =$ _____   **6.** $18 \div 3 =$ _____

7. $9 \div 3 =$ _____   **8.** $18 \div 2 =$ _____   **9.** $24 \div 3 =$ _____

10. $6 \div 2 =$ _____   **11.** $6 \div 3 =$ _____   **12.** $2 \div 2 =$ _____

13. $16 \div 2 =$ _____   **14.** $15 \div 3 =$ _____   **15.** $21 \div 3 =$ _____

16. $27 \div 3 =$ _____   **17.** $4 \div 2 =$ _____   **18.** $14 \div 2 =$ _____

19. $18 \div 2 =$ _____   **20.** $3 \div 3 =$ _____   **21.** $8 \div 2 =$ _____

22. $2 \div 2 =$ _____   **23.** $10 \div 2 =$ _____   **24.** $15 \div 3 =$ _____

25. Divide 27 by 3. _____   **26.** Divide 16 by 2. _____

27. Divide 9 by 3. _____   **28.** Divide 21 by 3. _____

29. Divide 6 by 2. _____   **30.** Divide 10 by 2. _____

Give the missing numbers.

31.
Divide by 2

10	8	6	14	16
5	4			

32.
Divide by 3

21	15	6	12	27
7	5			

Dividing by 4

Divide.

1. $24 \div 4 =$ _____

2. $12 \div 4 =$ _____

3. $6 \div 3 =$ _____

4. $20 \div 4 =$ _____

5. $2 \div 2 =$ _____

6. $36 \div 4 =$ _____

7. $14 \div 2 =$ _____

8. $28 \div 4 =$ _____

9. $8 \div 4 =$ _____

10. $24 \div 2 =$ _____

11. $3 \div 3 =$ _____

12. $18 \div 2 =$ _____

13. $36 \div 4 =$ _____

14. $20 \div 4 =$ _____

15. $32 \div 4 =$ _____

16. $9 \div 3 =$ _____

17. $4 \div 4 =$ _____

18. $12 \div 3 =$ _____

19. $12 \div 4 =$ _____

20. $4 \div 2 =$ _____

21. $16 \div 4 =$ _____

22. $20 \div 4 =$ _____

23. $36 \div 4 =$ _____

24. $16 \div 2 =$ _____

25. $6 \div 2 =$ _____

26. $24 \div 4 =$ _____

27. $4 \div 4 =$ _____

Is the missing number 2, 3, or 4?

28. $20 \div$ _____ $= 5$

29. $12 \div$ _____ $= 3$

30. $18 \div$ _____ $= 9$

31. $9 \div$ _____ $= 3$

32. $24 \div$ _____ $= 6$

33. $4 \div$ _____ $= 1$

Problem Solving: Using Data from a Graph

To solve some problems, you need to use data from a graph. Look at the graph Mike made as he watched vehicles drive past his house in one hour. Solve the problems using the data from the graph.

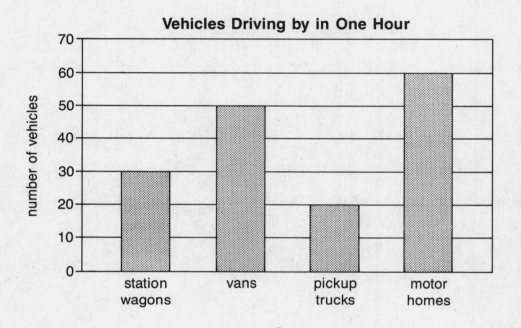

Vehicles Driving by in One Hour

1. How many vans went by in the hour?

   _____

2. How many station wagons went by?

   _____

3. What type of vehicle did Mike see the most?

   _____

4. What type of vehicle was double the number of station wagons?

   _____

5. How many more vans than station wagons went by?

   _____

6. How many vehicles of all types went by in 60 minutes?

   _____

Dividing by 5

Divide.

1. $10 \div 5 =$ _____ **2.** $9 \div 3 =$ _____ **3.** $15 \div 5 =$ _____

4. $6 \div 3 =$ _____ **5.** $25 \div 5 =$ _____ **6.** $5 \div 5 =$ _____

7. $12 \div 3 =$ _____ **8.** $40 \div 5 =$ _____ **9.** $10 \div 2 =$ _____

10. $45 \div 5 =$ _____ **11.** $20 \div 5 =$ _____ **12.** $3 \div 3 =$ _____

13. $36 \div 4 =$ _____ **14.** $8 \div 2 =$ _____ **15.** $20 \div 5 =$ _____

16. $20 \div 4 =$ _____ **17.** $30 \div 5 =$ _____ **18.** $25 \div 5 =$ _____

19. $15 \div 3 =$ _____ **20.** $12 \div 2 =$ _____ **21.** $24 \div 4 =$ _____

22. $35 \div 5 =$ _____ **23.** $8 \div 4 =$ _____ **24.** $40 \div 5 =$ _____

25. $20 \div 5 =$ _____ **26.** $18 \div 3 =$ _____ **27.** $10 \div 5 =$ _____

28. Divide 15 by 5. _____ **29.** Divide 18 by 2. _____

30. Divide 24 by 3. _____ **31.** Divide 40 by 5. _____

32. Divide 45 by 5. _____ **33.** Divide 28 by 4. _____

Mixed Practice

Choose a strategy you know to solve the problems.

Some Strategies	
Act It Out	Guess and Check
Use Objects	Make a Table
Choose an Operation	Look for a Pattern
Draw a Picture	Use Logical Reasoning
Make an Organized List	Work Backward

1. Kenny pitched 30 balls at practice. He pitched the same number of balls to each player. If 5 players batted, how many balls did Kenny pitch to each batter?

_____

2. Sue bought 5 softballs for the team. Each ball cost $4. How much did Sue spend?

_____

3. Tom, Marti, and Beth can pitch. Ruth and Pedro can catch. How many choices of pitcher and catcher does the coach have?

_____

4. Softball practice started at 6:15. The team did warm-up drills for 17 minutes. What time did they finish warm-ups?

_____

5. The coach threw ground balls to 7 players in the field. If she threw 9 balls to each fielder, how many balls did she throw?

_____

6. Beth used a target to practice pitching. On the first day she hit the target 5 times. On the second day she hit it 7 times. If she continues to improve at the same rate, how many times will she hit it on the fifth day?

_____

Name _____

Fact Families

Write a fact family for each set of factors
and products.

1. factor   factor
     3   9
        product
         27

_____

_____

_____

_____

2. factor   factor
     4   4
        product
         16

_____

_____

3. $3 \times 5 = 15$ _____

4. $3 \times 3 = 9$ _____

5. $2 \times 6 = 12$ _____

6. $4 \times 6 = 24$ _____

Find the missing fact family number. Then
write the complete fact family.

7.   2   ?
   factor   factor
       14
     product

_____

_____

8.   3   3
   factor   factor
       ?
     product

_____

_____

Name _____

0 and 1 in Division

Find the quotients.

1. $2\overline{)0}$ **2.** $1\overline{)0}$ **3.** $4\overline{)12}$ **4.** $5\overline{)30}$ **5.** $3\overline{)3}$

6. $1\overline{)7}$ **7.** $1\overline{)2}$ **8.** $3\overline{)12}$ **9.** $5\overline{)0}$ **10.** $4\overline{)24}$

11. $5\overline{)20}$ **12.** $4\overline{)0}$ **13.** $4\overline{)16}$ **14.** $5\overline{)35}$ **15.** $1\overline{)5}$

16. $5\overline{)5}$ **17.** $1\overline{)3}$ **18.** $3\overline{)15}$ **19.** $3\overline{)0}$ **20.** $5\overline{)15}$

21. $7\overline{)0}$ **22.** $5\overline{)40}$ **23.** $4\overline{)28}$ **24.** $3\overline{)21}$ **25.** $4\overline{)8}$

26. $6\overline{)0}$ **27.** $8\overline{)0}$ **28.** $8\overline{)8}$ **29.** $1\overline{)4}$ **30.** $9\overline{)0}$

31. $3\overline{)0}$ **32.** $9\overline{)9}$ **33.** $4\overline{)4}$ **34.** $5\overline{)25}$ **35.** $5\overline{)0}$

36. $1\overline{)6}$ **37.** $3\overline{)27}$ **38.** $4\overline{)16}$ **39.** $3\overline{)18}$ **40.** $2\overline{)4}$

41. $12 \div 2 =$ _____   **42.** $0 \div 4 =$ _____   **43.** $3 \div 1 =$ _____

44. $0 \div 7 =$ _____   **45.** $21 \div 3 =$ _____   **46.** $0 \div 1 =$ _____

47. $7 \div 7 =$ _____   **48.** $0 \div 5 =$ _____   **49.** $0 \div 2 =$ _____

Extending the Division Concept

Here is a list of the key actions that help you decide what operation to use to solve a problem.

ACTION	OPERATION
Put together	Add
Take away Compare Find a missing part	Subtract
Put together same- size sets	Multiply
Share a set equally Take away same-size sets repeatedly	Divide

Tell which action and operation you would use to solve the problem. Then solve.

1. There are 35 spinach plants in the garden. The plants are in 5 equal rows. How many spinach plants are in each row?

_____

_____

2. Joan bought some pencils for 42¢. Lorie bought some pencils for 54¢. How much money did the girls spend in all?

_____

_____

3. Rick earned $21 in 3 days. He earned an equal amount each day. How much did Rick earn each day?

_____

_____

4. Luis planted 6 rows of carrot seeds. There are 7 seeds in each row. How many carrot seeds did Luis plant?

_____

_____

Dividing by 6

Find the quotients.

1. $3\overline{)6}$ **2.** $6\overline{)12}$ **3.** $5\overline{)35}$ **4.** $6\overline{)48}$ **5.** $2\overline{)4}$

6. $6\overline{)42}$ **7.** $4\overline{)20}$ **8.** $6\overline{)36}$ **9.** $2\overline{)18}$ **10.** $4\overline{)28}$

11. $3\overline{)27}$ **12.** $3\overline{)12}$ **13.** $4\overline{)24}$ **14.** $3\overline{)9}$ **15.** $2\overline{)6}$

16. $5\overline{)30}$ **17.** $1\overline{)6}$ **18.** $2\overline{)8}$ **19.** $1\overline{)8}$ **20.** $2\overline{)10}$

21. $6\overline{)54}$ **22.** $3\overline{)15}$ **23.** $3\overline{)21}$ **24.** $2\overline{)12}$ **25.** $2\overline{)14}$

26. $6\overline{)18}$ **27.** $4\overline{)36}$ **28.** $4\overline{)32}$ **29.** $5\overline{)25}$ **30.** $6\overline{)6}$

31. $6\overline{)30}$ **32.** $5\overline{)45}$ **33.** $6\overline{)24}$ **34.** $3\overline{)18}$ **35.** $4\overline{)12}$

36. $5\overline{)20}$ **37.** $4\overline{)16}$ **38.** $3\overline{)24}$ **39.** $2\overline{)16}$ **40.** $1\overline{)5}$

41. $54 \div 6 =$ _____ **42.** $36 \div 6 =$ _____ **43.** $12 \div 6 =$ _____

44. $30 \div 6 =$ _____ **45.** $48 \div 6 =$ _____ **46.** $18 \div 6 =$ _____

47. $6 \div 6 =$ _____ **48.** $42 \div 6 =$ _____ **49.** $24 \div 6 =$ _____

Name _____

Dividing by 7

Divide.

1. $2\overline{)14}$ **2.** $3\overline{)24}$ **3.** $6\overline{)12}$ **4.** $4\overline{)24}$ **5.** $7\overline{)21}$

6. $1\overline{)7}$ **7.** $5\overline{)35}$ **8.** $1\overline{)2}$ **9.** $7\overline{)49}$ **10.** $6\overline{)30}$

11. $5\overline{)25}$ **12.** $4\overline{)28}$ **13.** $7\overline{)63}$ **14.** $3\overline{)27}$ **15.** $7\overline{)56}$

16. $2\overline{)18}$ **17.** $7\overline{)28}$ **18.** $3\overline{)21}$ **19.** $6\overline{)18}$ **20.** $2\overline{)8}$

21. $5\overline{)20}$ **22.** $6\overline{)54}$ **23.** $6\overline{)36}$ **24.** $4\overline{)36}$ **25.** $7\overline{)7}$

26. $2\overline{)2}$ **27.** $6\overline{)24}$ **28.** $1\overline{)8}$ **29.** $2\overline{)16}$ **30.** $7\overline{)35}$

31. $7\overline{)14}$ **32.** $7\overline{)42}$ **33.** $6\overline{)42}$ **34.** $2\overline{)12}$ **35.** $5\overline{)40}$

36. $4\overline{)32}$ **37.** $6\overline{)48}$ **38.** $3\overline{)18}$ **39.** $3\overline{)3}$ **40.** $5\overline{)15}$

41. $56 \div 7 =$ _____ **42.** $14 \div 7 =$ _____ **43.** $42 \div 7 =$ _____

44. $7 \div 1 =$ _____ **45.** $63 \div 7 =$ _____ **46.** $21 \div 7 =$ _____

47. $35 \div 7 =$ _____ **48.** $28 \div 7 =$ _____ **49.** $49 \div 7 =$ _____

Finding Related Problems

The table shows the kinds of displays at the school science fair. It also shows how many displays there were of each kind.

Decide whether you need to use the data from the table. Then solve the problems.

Kind of Display	Number of Displays
animals	14
plants	18
rocks	5
weather	6
space	24
electricity	9
other	12
Total	88

1. Pam had a display about animals. How many other displays were about animals?

   _____

2. How many more displays were about space than about plants?

   _____

3. The plant displays were divided into 2 equal groups. How many were in each group?

   _____

4. Kelly had a shell display. She put her 45 shells into 5 equal rows. How many shells were in each row?

   _____

5. One of the plant displays had 8 pots of plants. Each pot had 2 plants in it. How many plants were in that display?

   _____

6. The rock, weather, space, and electricity displays were in the multipurpose room. How many displays were in the multipurpose room?

   _____

7. Joe brought a bag of rocks for his display. He put out 6 rocks in each of 5 rows. There were 12 rocks left in the bag. How many were in the bag when Joe brought it?

   _____

Name _____

Exploring Algebra

You can replace the △ and □ with pairs of
numbers to make true equations. In the
tables, list in order the ways you can
replace the △ and □.

1.　△ − □ = 1

9	8	9, 8

2.　△ + □ = 9

0	9	0, 9
1	8	1, 8

3. Next to Exercises 1 and 2, write each of the number pairs in the tables
as an ordered pair. Use this order (△ , □).

4. Make a point on the graph for
each ordered pair in Exercise 1.
Use a red pencil to connect the
points in the graph.

5. Make a point on the graph for
each ordered pair in Exercise 2.
Use a blue pencil to connect
the points in the graph.

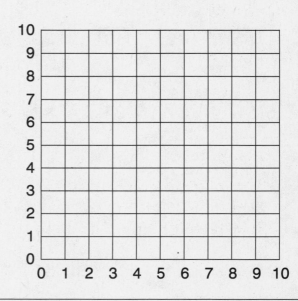

Name _____

Dividing by 8

Divide.

1. $8\overline{)8}$ **2.** $2\overline{)16}$ **3.** $7\overline{)14}$ **4.** $4\overline{)32}$ **5.** $8\overline{)48}$

6. $6\overline{)24}$ **7.** $7\overline{)42}$ **8.** $6\overline{)42}$ **9.** $3\overline{)18}$ **10.** $3\overline{)12}$

11. $5\overline{)40}$ **12.** $2\overline{)14}$ **13.** $8\overline{)40}$ **14.** $3\overline{)24}$ **15.** $8\overline{)32}$

16. $4\overline{)36}$ **17.** $7\overline{)21}$ **18.** $8\overline{)16}$ **19.** $5\overline{)5}$ **20.** $3\overline{)15}$

21. $8\overline{)72}$ **22.** $6\overline{)12}$ **23.** $7\overline{)49}$ **24.** $7\overline{)28}$ **25.** $6\overline{)48}$

26. $8\overline{)64}$ **27.** $1\overline{)8}$ **28.** $7\overline{)56}$ **29.** $6\overline{)30}$ **30.** $5\overline{)30}$

31. $4\overline{)24}$ **32.** $2\overline{)10}$ **33.** $5\overline{)25}$ **34.** $8\overline{)24}$ **35.** $4\overline{)28}$

36. $6\overline{)54}$ **37.** $7\overline{)35}$ **38.** $8\overline{)56}$ **39.** $3\overline{)27}$ **40.** $6\overline{)36}$

41. $8 \div 8 =$ _____ **42.** $32 \div 8 =$ _____ **43.** $64 \div 8 =$ _____

44. $72 \div 8 =$ _____ **45.** $16 \div 8 =$ _____ **46.** $40 \div 8 =$ _____

47. $24 \div 8 =$ _____ **48.** $56 \div 8 =$ _____ **49.** $48 \div 8 =$ _____

Name _____

Dividing by 9

Divide.

1. $9 \overline{)9}$ **2.** $5 \overline{)25}$ **3.** $8 \overline{)56}$ **4.** $9 \overline{)36}$ **5.** $4 \overline{)20}$

6. $9 \overline{)54}$ **7.** $8 \overline{)64}$ **8.** $1 \overline{)9}$ **9.** $3 \overline{)21}$ **10.** $9 \overline{)72}$

11. $3 \overline{)27}$ **12.** $7 \overline{)49}$ **13.** $2 \overline{)16}$ **14.** $8 \overline{)72}$ **15.** $7 \overline{)63}$

16. $9 \overline{)63}$ **17.** $8 \overline{)8}$ **18.** $2 \overline{)14}$ **19.** $9 \overline{)27}$ **20.** $4 \overline{)36}$

21. $6 \overline{)48}$ **22.** $6 \overline{)36}$ **23.** $9 \overline{)45}$ **24.** $4 \overline{)24}$ **25.** $2 \overline{)18}$

26. $3 \overline{)12}$ **27.** $1 \overline{)7}$ **28.** $3 \overline{)6}$ **29.** $6 \overline{)42}$ **30.** $4 \overline{)28}$

31. $6 \overline{)54}$ **32.** $5 \overline{)45}$ **33.** $4 \overline{)16}$ **34.** $9 \overline{)81}$ **35.** $5 \overline{)10}$

36. $7 \overline{)42}$ **37.** $5 \overline{)40}$ **38.** $9 \overline{)18}$ **39.** $5 \overline{)35}$ **40.** $7 \overline{)56}$

41. $9 \div 1 = $ _____   **42.** $36 \div 9 = $ _____   **43.** $45 \div 9 = $ _____

44. $63 \div 9 = $ _____   **45.** $18 \div 9 = $ _____   **46.** $27 \div 9 = $ _____

47. $72 \div 9 = $ _____   **48.** $81 \div 9 = $ _____   **49.** $54 \div 9 = $ _____

Know Your Facts

Give these quotients as quickly as you can.
Use what you know about patterns to help you.

1. $54 \div 9 =$ _____   **2.** $27 \div 3 =$ _____   **3.** $21 \div 7 =$ _____

4. $18 \div 3 =$ _____   **5.** $24 \div 3 =$ _____   **6.** $16 \div 8 =$ _____

7. $20 \div 5 =$ _____   **8.** $12 \div 4 =$ _____   **9.** $24 \div 8 =$ _____

10. $54 \div 9 =$ _____   **11.** $42 \div 7 =$ _____   **12.** $24 \div 4 =$ _____

13. Divide 36 by 9. _____

14. What is 45 divided by 5? _____

15. What is 63 divided by 7? _____

16. What is 36 divided by 9? _____

17. $6\overline{)24}$ **18.** $8\overline{)72}$ **19.** $6\overline{)48}$ **20.** $8\overline{)48}$

21. $3\overline{)18}$ **22.** $9\overline{)45}$ **23.** $6\overline{)42}$ **24.** $7\overline{)35}$

25. $6\overline{)54}$ **26.** $8\overline{)64}$ **27.** $6\overline{)36}$ **28.** $9\overline{)63}$

29. $9\overline{)81}$ **30.** $7\overline{)49}$ **31.** $7\overline{)56}$ **32.** $9\overline{)72}$

Multiply and Then Add

Multiply and then add 1. Write answers only.

1. 4×2 _____

2. 2×1 _____

3. 7×6 _____

4. 5×0 _____

5. 2×5 _____

6. 3×3 _____

Multiply and then add 2. Write answers only.

7. 6×2 _____

8. 4×7 _____

9. 3×4 _____

10. 4×9 _____

11. 0×3 _____

12. 5×5 _____

Find the product and then add 3. Write answers only.

13. 8×4 _____

14. 5×2 _____

15. 6×3 _____

16. 3×3 _____

17. 9×3 _____

18. 8×0 _____

Find the product and then add 4. Write answers only.

19. 1×6 _____

20. 9×8 _____

21. 7×3 _____

22. 9×7 _____

23. 0×6 _____

24. 8×7 _____

Multiply the first two numbers. Then add the product
to the third number. Write answers only.

25. 6, 7, 4 _____

26. 7, 7, 1 _____

27. 3, 7, 2 _____

28. 4, 7, 3 _____

29. 2, 7, 5 _____

30. 5, 7, 4 _____

Name _____

Special Products

1. Find the product of 20 and 8.   **2.** Find the product of 6 and 30.

_____   _____

3. Multiply 50 by 9.   **4.** Multiply 70 by 3.

_____   _____

Estimate products by breaking apart numbers into tens.

5. 13×10 _____   **6.** 6×40 _____   **7.** 45×10 _____

8. 4×20 _____   **9.** 17×10 _____   **10.** 2×60 _____

Multiply.

11. 2×90 _____   **12.** 7×60 _____   **13.** 4×50 _____

14. 3×30 _____   **15.** 4×30 _____   **16.** 8×50 _____

17. 5×20 _____   **18.** 9×40 _____   **19.** 6×70 _____

20. $\begin{array}{r} 80 \\ \times\ 6 \\ \hline \end{array}$ **21.** $\begin{array}{r} 40 \\ \times\ 7 \\ \hline \end{array}$ **22.** $\begin{array}{r} 60 \\ \times\ 3 \\ \hline \end{array}$ **23.** $\begin{array}{r} 50 \\ \times\ 9 \\ \hline \end{array}$

24. $\begin{array}{r} 20 \\ \times\ 4 \\ \hline \end{array}$ **25.** $\begin{array}{r} 70 \\ \times\ 2 \\ \hline \end{array}$ **26.** $\begin{array}{r} 30 \\ \times\ 5 \\ \hline \end{array}$ **27.** $\begin{array}{r} 40 \\ \times\ 8 \\ \hline \end{array}$

Estimating Products Using Rounding

Estimate each product by rounding to the nearest
ten. Tell whether the exact product is over or
under your estimate.

1. 88
$\times$ 5

2. 29
$\times$ 3

3. 38
$\times$ 8

4. 19
$\times$ 4

5. 4×31

6. 6×42

7. 9×29

8. 5×64

9. 3×39

10. 8×73

11. 7×44

12. 6×68

Estimate the product. Is it more or less than the
reference point in parentheses?

13. 2×48 (100)

14. 8×21 (160)

15. 5×36 (200)

16. 7×84 (560)

17. 4×89 (360)

18. 6×34 (180)

19. 3×22 (60)

20. 8×78 (640)

21. 4×43 (160)

22. 2×47 (100)

23. 4×57 (240)

24. 7×56 (420)

Multiplying: Making the Connection

1. One pencil costs 14¢. With play money, show
how much 3 pencils will cost.
Put out 1 dime and 4 pennies for each pencil.

Are there enough pennies to trade? _____

How many pennies are there after the trade?_____

How many dimes are there after the trade? _____

What is the product of 3 × 14¢? _____

Use play money to practice multiplication with trading.

2. 4 times 14¢

_____

3. 3 times 15¢

_____

4. 2 times 25¢

_____

5. 4 times 16¢

_____

6. Amy bought 4 stamps for 15¢
each. How much did she pay?

_____

7. Neal bought 3 stamps for 25¢
each. How much did he pay?

_____

Circle the examples where you must trade to find the
answer. Do not solve.

8.	**9.**	**10.**	**11.**	**12.**
45	29	30	25	21
× 4	× 2	× 3	× 2	× 4

Multiplying: Trading Ones

Decide if you need to trade. Then find the products.

1. $\begin{array}{r} 12 \\ \times\ 3 \\ \hline \end{array}$
   2. $\begin{array}{r} 24 \\ \times\ 2 \\ \hline \end{array}$
   3. $\begin{array}{r} 11 \\ \times\ 8 \\ \hline \end{array}$
   4. $\begin{array}{r} 29 \\ \times\ 3 \\ \hline \end{array}$
   5. $\begin{array}{r} 13 \\ \times\ 3 \\ \hline \end{array}$

6. $\begin{array}{r} 46 \\ \times\ 2 \\ \hline \end{array}$
   7. $\begin{array}{r} 22 \\ \times\ 4 \\ \hline \end{array}$
   8. $\begin{array}{r} 19 \\ \times\ 4 \\ \hline \end{array}$
   9. $\begin{array}{r} 12 \\ \times\ 8 \\ \hline \end{array}$
   10. $\begin{array}{r} 30 \\ \times\ 2 \\ \hline \end{array}$

11. $\begin{array}{r} 15 \\ \times\ 5 \\ \hline \end{array}$
   12. $\begin{array}{r} 12 \\ \times\ 7 \\ \hline \end{array}$
   13. $\begin{array}{r} 20 \\ \times\ 4 \\ \hline \end{array}$
   14. $\begin{array}{r} 19 \\ \times\ 5 \\ \hline \end{array}$
   15. $\begin{array}{r} 26 \\ \times\ 2 \\ \hline \end{array}$

Multiply.

16. 3×25 **17.** 6×13 **18.** 4×24 **19.** 5×12

20. 7×12 **21.** 2×20 **22.** 4×22 **23.** 8×12

24. What is 15 multiplied by 5?   **25.** Find the product of 18 and 3.

_____   _____

Name _____

More About Multiplying

Find the products.

1. $\begin{array}{r} 12 \\ \times\ 5 \\ \hline \end{array}$
  2. $\begin{array}{r} 11 \\ \times\ 9 \\ \hline \end{array}$
  3. $\begin{array}{r} 14 \\ \times\ 7 \\ \hline \end{array}$
  4. $\begin{array}{r} 24 \\ \times\ 4 \\ \hline \end{array}$
  5. $\begin{array}{r} 13 \\ \times\ 7 \\ \hline \end{array}$

6. $\begin{array}{r} 42 \\ \times\ 2 \\ \hline \end{array}$
  7. $\begin{array}{r} 14 \\ \times\ 6 \\ \hline \end{array}$
  8. $\begin{array}{r} 28 \\ \times\ 2 \\ \hline \end{array}$
  9. $\begin{array}{r} 23 \\ \times\ 4 \\ \hline \end{array}$
  10. $\begin{array}{r} 12 \\ \times\ 4 \\ \hline \end{array}$

11. $\begin{array}{r} 12 \\ \times\ 2 \\ \hline \end{array}$
  12. $\begin{array}{r} 18 \\ \times\ 2 \\ \hline \end{array}$
  13. $\begin{array}{r} 53 \\ \times\ 4 \\ \hline \end{array}$
  14. $\begin{array}{r} 61 \\ \times\ 3 \\ \hline \end{array}$
  15. $\begin{array}{r} 37 \\ \times\ 6 \\ \hline \end{array}$

Multiply.

16. 5×39 **17.** 48×7 **18.** 29×5 **19.** 25×6

20. 8×67 **21.** 7×53 **22.** 8×74 **23.** 5×72

24. What is 16 multiplied by 8?   **25.** Find the product of 15 and 4.

_____   _____

Name _____

Using Critical Thinking

Find the missing digits.

1.
$$\begin{array}{r} \boxed{}\,1 \\ \times \quad \boxed{} \\ \hline 6\ 3 \end{array}$$

2.
$$\begin{array}{r} \boxed{}\,2 \\ \times \quad 4 \\ \hline 1\ 2\ \boxed{} \end{array}$$

3.
$$\begin{array}{r} {}^{1}\ 6\ 3 \\ \times \quad \boxed{} \\ \hline \boxed{}\,\boxed{}\,8 \end{array}$$

4.
$$\begin{array}{r} {}^{4}\,\boxed{}\,8 \\ \times \quad \boxed{} \\ \hline 9\ 0 \end{array}$$

5.
$$\begin{array}{r} {}^{1}\,\boxed{}\,4 \\ \times \quad 4 \\ \hline 1\ 7\ \boxed{} \end{array}$$

6.
$$\begin{array}{r} {}^{1}\,\boxed{}\,8 \\ \times \quad \boxed{} \\ \hline \boxed{}\,3\ 6 \end{array}$$

7.
$$\begin{array}{r} \boxed{}\,1 \\ \times \quad \boxed{} \\ \hline 2\ \boxed{}\,9 \end{array}$$

8.
$$\begin{array}{r} {}^{3}\ 2\ 7 \\ \times \quad \boxed{} \\ \hline \boxed{}\,\boxed{}\,5 \end{array}$$

9.
$$\begin{array}{r} {}^{1}\ 1\ \boxed{} \\ \times \quad 8 \\ \hline 9\ \boxed{} \end{array}$$

10.
$$\begin{array}{r} {}^{4}\ 3\ \boxed{} \\ \times \quad 6 \\ \hline \boxed{}\,2\ 2 \end{array}$$

11.
$$\begin{array}{r} 4\ \boxed{} \\ \times \quad 8 \\ \hline 3\ \boxed{}\,0 \end{array}$$

12.
$$\begin{array}{r} {}^{2}\,\boxed{}\,3 \\ \times \quad \boxed{} \\ \hline \boxed{}\,6\ 1 \end{array}$$

13.
$$\begin{array}{r} {}^{2}\ 1\ \boxed{} \\ \times \quad 5 \\ \hline 7\ \boxed{} \end{array}$$

14.
$$\begin{array}{r} {}^{1}\ 5\ \boxed{} \\ \times \quad 3 \\ \hline \boxed{}\,\boxed{}\,2 \end{array}$$

15.
$$\begin{array}{r} \boxed{}\,1 \\ \times \quad 6 \\ \hline 4\ 2\ \boxed{} \end{array}$$

Choosing a Calculation Method

To calculate an answer to a problem, you can use mental math, paper and pencil, or a calculator. Tell which calculation method you would use and why. Then solve. Use each method at least twice.

1.
$$\begin{array}{r} 50 \\ \times\ 7 \\ \hline \end{array}$$

Method: _____

Reason: _____

2.
$$\begin{array}{r} 866 \\ \times\ \ \ 2 \\ \hline \end{array}$$

Method: _____

Reason: _____

3.
$$\begin{array}{r} 75 \\ \times\ 4 \\ \hline \end{array}$$

Method: _____

Reason: _____

4. 7×12

Method: _____

Reason: _____

5. 6×9

Method: _____

Reason: _____

6. $68 - 32$

Method: _____

Reason: _____

7.
$$\begin{array}{r} \$8.50 \\ -\ 3.50 \\ \hline \end{array}$$

Method: _____

Reason: _____

8.
$$\begin{array}{r} \$5.97 \\ -\ 1.21 \\ \hline \end{array}$$

Method: _____

Reason: _____

9.
$$\begin{array}{r} \$239.68 \\ -\ 219.68 \\ \hline \end{array}$$

Method: _____

Reason: _____

10. 7×10

Method: _____

Reason: _____

11. $85 - 47$

Method: _____

Reason: _____

12. 3×789

Method: _____

Reason: _____

Estimating and Finding Money Products

Estimate the products. Then find the exact answers.

1. 7 × $0.79

2. 8 × $0.26

3. 3 × $0.48

4. 5 × $0.42

5. 6 × $0.59

6. 9 × $0.93

7.
$$\begin{array}{r} \$0.49 \\ \times\ \ \ \ 7 \\ \hline \end{array}$$

8.
$$\begin{array}{r} \$0.72 \\ \times\ \ \ \ 5 \\ \hline \end{array}$$

9.
$$\begin{array}{r} \$0.66 \\ \times\ \ \ \ 3 \\ \hline \end{array}$$

10.
$$\begin{array}{r} \$0.54 \\ \times\ \ \ \ 4 \\ \hline \end{array}$$

11.
$$\begin{array}{r} \$0.17 \\ \times\ \ \ \ 8 \\ \hline \end{array}$$

12.
$$\begin{array}{r} \$0.39 \\ \times\ \ \ \ 9 \\ \hline \end{array}$$

13.
$$\begin{array}{r} \$0.24 \\ \times\ \ \ \ 6 \\ \hline \end{array}$$

14.
$$\begin{array}{r} \$0.88 \\ \times\ \ \ \ 5 \\ \hline \end{array}$$

15.
$$\begin{array}{r} \$0.77 \\ \times\ \ \ \ 4 \\ \hline \end{array}$$

16.
$$\begin{array}{r} \$0.51 \\ \times\ \ \ \ 7 \\ \hline \end{array}$$

17.
$$\begin{array}{r} \$0.34 \\ \times\ \ \ \ 8 \\ \hline \end{array}$$

18.
$$\begin{array}{r} \$0.14 \\ \times\ \ \ \ 9 \\ \hline \end{array}$$

19. 7 at $0.73 each

20. 6 at $0.19 each

21. 3 at $0.95 each

22. 4 at $0.86 each

23. 9 at $0.28 each

24. 5 at $0.53 each

Using a Calculator

Solve. You may use a calculator.

1. Yesterday Mr. Burns sold 3 boxes with 100 nails in each box, 5 boxes with 275 nails, and 2 boxes with 1,000 nails. How many nails did Mr. Burns sell in all?

_____

2. For a customer, Mr. Sanchez made 25 copies of 2 papers, 43 copies of 4 papers, and 61 copies of 1 paper. How many copies did Mr. Sanchez make in all?

_____

3. Brad needed to store toys on shelves. 5 toys could fit on each shelf. There were 8 shelves. How many toys could Brad store?

_____

4. Elsie paid $2.19 for a package of paper, $0.80 for some paper clips, and she bought 2 pens for $0.40 each. How much change did Elsie get from a ten-dollar bills?

_____

5. Juanita wants to buy a calculator. She can choose from two brands, Speedy and Electric City. Each brand has four different models, A, B, C, and D. How many different calculators can Juanita choose from?

_____

6. Mrs. Earl bought 4 yards of ribbon for her sewing project. The ribbon was $0.79 per yard. How much did Mrs. Earl pay for the ribbon?

_____

Estimating and Measuring Length in Centimeters

A paper clip is about 3 centimeters (cm) long. Use the paper clip as a benchmark to make these estimates. Check your estimates by measuring to the nearest centimeter.

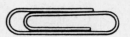

1. Length of your thumb

_____

2. Width of your math book

_____

3. Length of a crayon

_____

4. Length of a pencil

_____

5. Length of an envelope

_____

6. Length of a safety pin

_____

Use your hand span as a benchmark to estimate these lengths. Check your estimates by measuring to the nearest centimeter.

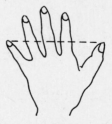

7. Length from wrist to elbow

_____

8. Length from ankle to knee

_____

9. Width of a notebook

_____

10. Length of a chalkboard eraser

_____

Decimeter, Meter, and Kilometer

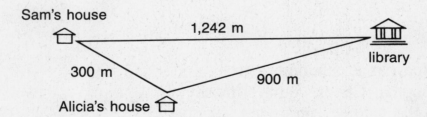

200 cm

0.50 cm

20 cm

PAINT

30 cm

25 cm

6 cm

Use these pictures to help answer the questions.

1. Which object is shorter than 1 cm? _____

2. Which objects are longer than 1 dm? _____

_____

3. Which object is longer than 1 m? _____

Sam's house

1,242 m

library

300 m

900 m

Alicia's house

4. Which distance is greater than 1 kilometer? _____

_____

5. Which distances are less than 1 kilometer? _____

_____

Name _____

Area

Give the area of each shape in square centimeters.

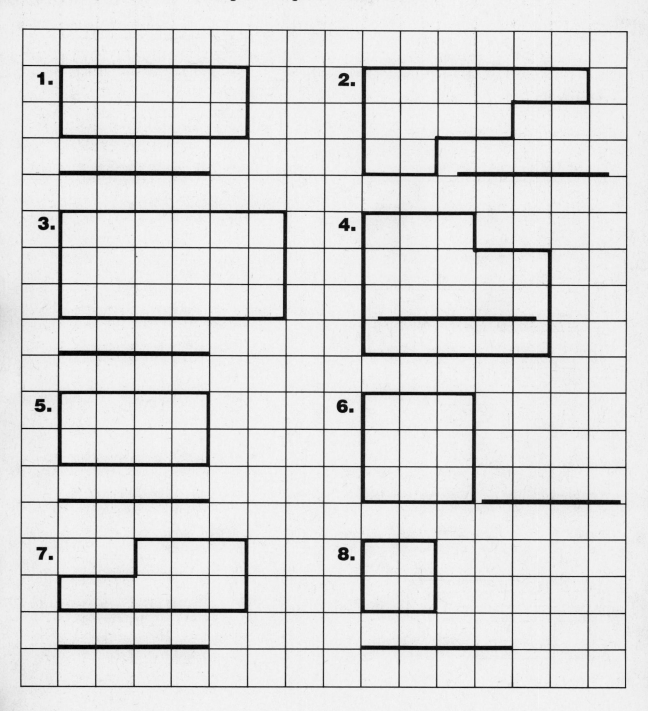

Volume

Find the volume of each figure in cubic units.

1.

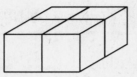

_____

2.

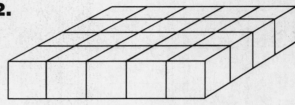

_____

3.

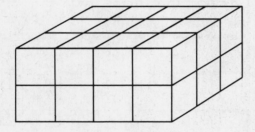

_____

4.

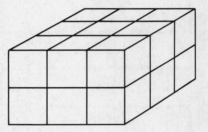

_____

5.

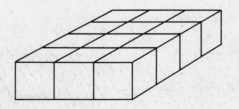

_____

6.

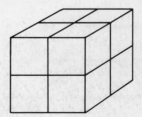

_____

Name _____

Temperature

Record each temperature.

1.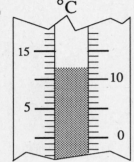

2.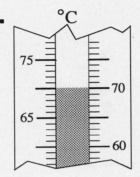

3.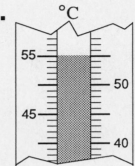

4.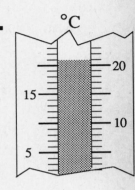

_____   _____   _____   _____

5.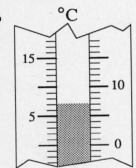

6.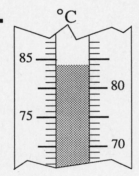

7.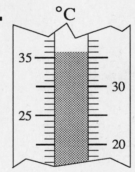

8.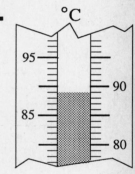

_____   _____   _____   _____

Fill in each thermometer to the correct temperature.

9. 65°C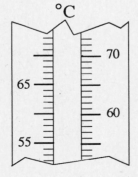

10. 14°C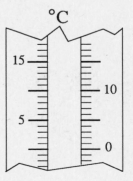

Liters and Milliliters

Use this benchmark to estimate whether the object holds **more** than, **less** than, or about the **same** as 1 liter.

An orange juice carton holds 1 L.

1.

_____

2.

_____

3.

_____

4.

_____

5.

_____

6.

_____

Use this benchmark to estimate whether the object holds **more** than, **less** than, or about the **same** as 1 milliliter.

A medicine dropper holds about 1 mL.

7.

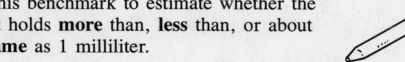

_____

8.

_____

9.

_____

Grams and Kilograms

Work with a partner. Use benchmarks to estimate the weight of these objects in grams or kilograms. Then weigh each object on a metric scale.

paper clip 1 g

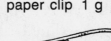

math book 1 kg

1. Roll of tape

estimate: _____

weight: _____

2. 10 rubber bands

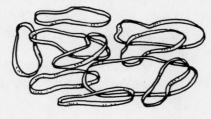

estimate: _____

weight: _____

3. Paper bag

estimate: _____

weight: _____

4. Encyclopedia

estimate: _____

weight: _____

5. Running shoes

estimate: _____

weight: _____

6. Wastebasket

estimate: _____

weight: _____

7. Calculator

estimate: _____

weight: _____

8. 3 pencils

estimate: _____

weight: _____

9. Scissors

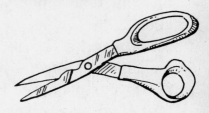

estimate: _____

weight: _____

Deciding When to Estimate

Read each problem. Write whether you can estimate
or whether you need to measure.

1. Your goldfish need to have
1 gram of food at each feeding.
Should you measure or estimate?

_____

2. The directions for painting a
ceiling say never to paint
more than 2 feet at a time. If
you are painting, should you
measure or estimate?

_____

Choose a strategy you know to solve these
problems.

3. Your mother needs to buy
boards to build a fence. She
needs 4 boards that are 5 feet
long and 6 boards that are
3 feet long. If boards cost $1
per foot, how much will the
boards cost in all?

_____

4. There are 8 houses on each
block near the school. There
are 6 blocks in all. If you want
each house to get a flier about
the school fair, how many do
you need to make?

_____

5. The hinges on a door have
broken. One hinge you need
costs $4.98 and another costs
$3.50. You also need to buy 2
packages of special nails at
$2.00 per package. How much
will it cost to repair the door?

_____

6. Mrs. Miller started her exercise
program slowly. She walked
1,000 meters each day of week
1, 1,200 meters each day of week
2, and 1,400 meters each day
of week 3. If her pattern continues,
how far will Mrs. Miller walk
each day of week 5?

_____

Naming Parts of a Whole

Ring the name of the parts of each whole.

1.

A halves

B thirds

C fourths

D not given

2.
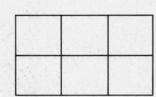

A halves

B fourths

C sixths

D not given

3.
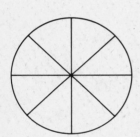

A fifths

B eighths

C tenths

D not given

4.

A halves

B thirds

C sixths

D not given

5.
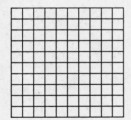

A eighths

B tenths

C hundredths

D not given

6.
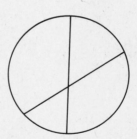

A halves

B thirds

C fourths

D not given

7.
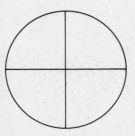

A halves

B fourths

C eighths

D not given

8.
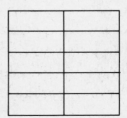

A eighths

B tenths

C hundredths

D not given

Understanding Fractions

Answer each question by writing a fraction.

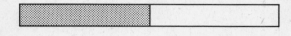

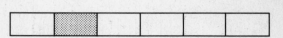

1. How much is shaded? $\frac{1}{2}$

How much is not shaded? $\frac{1}{2}$

2. How much is shaded? _____

How much is not shaded? ____

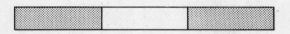

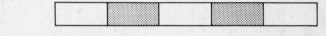

3. How much is shaded? _____

How much is not shaded? ____

4. How much is shaded? _____

How much is not shaded? ____

5. Shade $\frac{3}{4}$ of this strip.

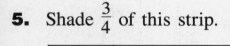

6. Shade $\frac{2}{3}$ of this strip.

7. Shade $\frac{1}{4}$ of this strip.

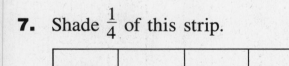

8. Shade $\frac{4}{5}$ of this strip.

Write the fraction that tells what part is shaded.

9.

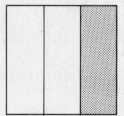

10.

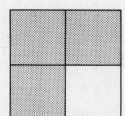

11.

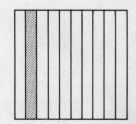

_____   _____   _____

Equivalent Fractions

Write the missing fraction.

1.

$$\frac{1}{2} = \rule{2cm}{0.4pt}$$

2.

$$\frac{2}{4} = \rule{2cm}{0.4pt}$$

3.

$$\frac{1}{5} = \rule{2cm}{0.4pt}$$

4.

$$\frac{3}{4} = \rule{2cm}{0.4pt}$$

5.

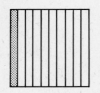

$$\frac{1}{10} = \rule{2cm}{0.4pt}$$

6.

$$\frac{4}{8} = \rule{2cm}{0.4pt}$$

7.

$$\frac{2}{3} = \rule{2cm}{0.4pt}$$

8.

$$\frac{1}{4} = \rule{2cm}{0.4pt}$$

Name _____

Comparing Fractions

The strips at the right will help you compare fractions.

Write, >, <, or = in each ◯.

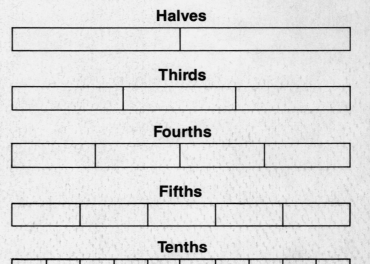

Halves

Thirds

Fourths

Fifths

Tenths

1. $\frac{1}{2}$ ◯ $\frac{1}{3}$

2. $\frac{1}{2}$ ◯ $\frac{2}{4}$

3. $\frac{1}{5}$ ◯ $\frac{1}{4}$

4. $\frac{3}{10}$ ◯ $\frac{1}{4}$ **5.** $\frac{1}{3}$ ◯ $\frac{1}{10}$ **6.** $\frac{3}{5}$ ◯ $\frac{6}{10}$

7. $\frac{1}{2}$ ◯ $\frac{2}{5}$ **8.** $\frac{3}{5}$ ◯ $\frac{2}{3}$ **9.** $\frac{2}{4}$ ◯ $\frac{5}{10}$

10. $\frac{1}{3}$ ◯ $\frac{1}{5}$ **11.** $\frac{4}{5}$ ◯ $\frac{8}{10}$ **12.** $\frac{1}{5}$ ◯ $\frac{1}{10}$

13. $\frac{1}{5}$ ◯ $\frac{2}{10}$ **14.** $\frac{1}{5}$ ◯ $\frac{3}{10}$ **15.** $\frac{1}{4}$ ◯ $\frac{1}{3}$

16. $\frac{1}{2}$ ◯ $\frac{5}{10}$ **17.** $\frac{3}{4}$ ◯ $\frac{2}{3}$ **18.** $\frac{3}{4}$ ◯ $\frac{7}{10}$

Fractional Part of a Set

Write the fraction of the glasses that are filled.

1.

_____

2.

_____

3.

_____

4.

_____

5.

_____

6.

_____

7.

_____

8.

_____

Name _____

Finding a Fraction of a Number

Find each of the following.

1. $\frac{1}{4}$ of 36 _____

2. $\frac{1}{5}$ of 50 _____

3. $\frac{1}{7}$ of 42 _____

4. $\frac{1}{8}$ of 16 _____

5. $\frac{1}{5}$ of 25 _____

6. $\frac{1}{8}$ of 72 _____

7. $\frac{1}{3}$ of 15 _____

8. $\frac{1}{6}$ of 36 _____

9. $\frac{1}{9}$ of 45 _____

10. $\frac{1}{10}$ of 60 _____

11. $\frac{1}{3}$ of 9 _____

12. $\frac{1}{9}$ of 81 _____

13. $\frac{1}{7}$ of 7 _____

14. $\frac{1}{4}$ of 20 _____

15. $\frac{1}{2}$ of 6 _____

16. $\frac{1}{5}$ of 45 _____

17. $\frac{1}{8}$ of 56 _____

18. $\frac{1}{3}$ of 18 _____

19. $\frac{1}{8}$ of 32 _____

20. $\frac{1}{7}$ of 28 _____

21. $\frac{1}{6}$ of 30 _____

22. $\frac{1}{2}$ of 2 _____

23. $\frac{1}{4}$ of 8 _____

24. $\frac{1}{5}$ of 35 _____

Name _____

Exploring Algebra

1. Use objects or draw pictures on paper to make the next two designs. Then complete the table.

What is the number pattern in the table?

_____

_____

Use a calculator to find the number of blocks in the fifteenth design.

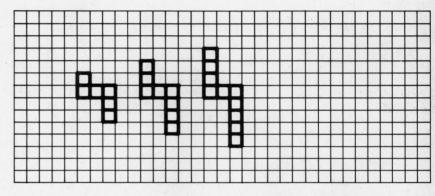

Design Number	1st	2nd	3rd	4th	5th	6th
Number of Blocks	6	8	10			

_____

2. Use objects or draw pictures on paper to make the next two designs. Then complete the table.

What is the number pattern in the table?

_____

_____

Use a calculator to find the number of blocks in the fifteenth design.

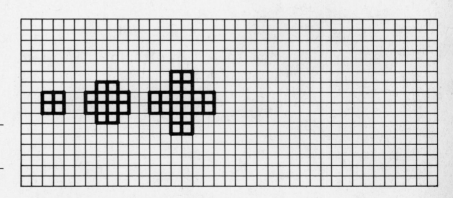

Design Number	1st	2nd	3rd	4th	5th	6th
Number of Blocks	4	12	20			

_____

Estimating Fractional Parts

Estimate how much is in each container.
Compare to the benchmarks.

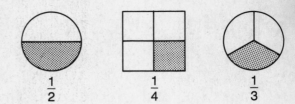

$\frac{1}{2}$ $\frac{1}{4}$ $\frac{1}{3}$

1.   **2.**   **3.**    **4.**

_____   _____   _____   _____

5.    **6.**    **7.**    **8.**

_____   _____   _____   _____

Color each container to match the fraction below it.

9.   **10.**   **11.**   **12.**

About $\frac{1}{3}$ About $\frac{3}{4}$ About $\frac{1}{4}$ About $\frac{1}{2}$
full   full   full   full

Mixed Numbers

Write a mixed number for each picture.

1.

_____

2.

_____

3.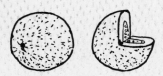

_____

4.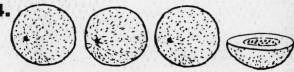

_____

Draw a line segment for each of the following.

5. $4\frac{1}{4}$ in.

6. $5\frac{3}{4}$ in.

Give each length.

7.

_____

8.

_____

Adding and Subtracting Fractions

Find each sum or difference.

1. $\frac{2}{4} + \frac{1}{4} = $ _____

2. $\frac{3}{5} - \frac{1}{5} = $ _____

3. $\frac{8}{10} - \frac{4}{10} = $ _____

4. $\frac{7}{10} + \frac{2}{10} = $ _____

5. $\frac{6}{8} - \frac{2}{8} = $ _____

6. $\frac{5}{6} - \frac{3}{6} = $ _____

7. $\frac{10}{12} - \frac{6}{12} = $ _____

8. $\frac{3}{8} + \frac{2}{8} = $ _____

9. $\frac{7}{12} + \frac{2}{12} = $ _____

Write a fraction equation for each action.
Then solve the equation.

10. Take 1 fourth from 3 fourths.

11. Put 2 sixths with 3 sixths.

12. Find how many more 7 tenths is than 2 tenths.

13. Take 5 eighths away from 7 eighths.

14. Put 3 fifths with 1 fifth.

15. Take 1 third from 2 thirds.

Name _____

Reading and Writing Decimals

Write a decimal for the shaded part of each set of books or figure.

1.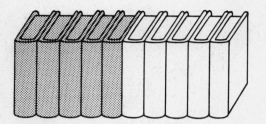

_____

2.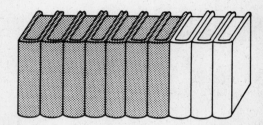

_____

3.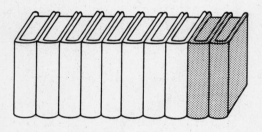

_____

4.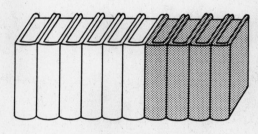

_____

5.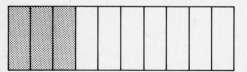

_____

6.

_____

7. Draw and shade 0.4 of a figure.

Larger Decimals

Read and write a decimal for each graph-paper model.

1.

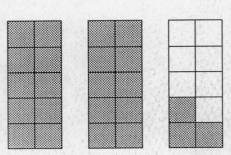

_____

2.

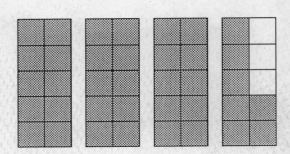

_____

3.

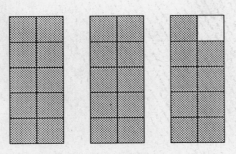

_____

4.

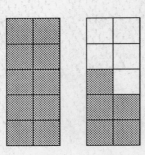

_____

Draw a model for each of the following.

5. 3.5

6. 1.8

Extending Decimal Concepts

Write a decimal for each.

1. Six and forty-six hundredths

_____

2. Four and eighty hundredths

_____

3. Fourteen and twenty-six hundredths

_____

4. Nine and seventy-five hundredths

_____

5. Three and seventy hundredths

_____

6. Sixteen and forty-one hundredths

_____

Work with a partner. Write a decimal to tell how much is shaded. Have your partner show the decimal on a calculator. Take turns.

7.

_____

8.

_____

9.

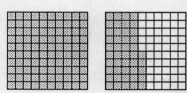

_____

10.

_____

11.

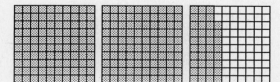

_____

12.

_____

Adding and Subtracting Decimals: Making the Connection

Use place-value blocks to add or subtract.

1. Add 2.3 and 4.5.

2. Add 6.7 and 1.6.

_____

3. Subtract 1.4 from 5.6.

4. Subtract 2.3 from 7.8.

_____

_____

Find the sums.

5. $\begin{array}{r} 3.4 \\ +\ 2.5 \\ \hline \end{array}$	**6.** $\begin{array}{r} 2.6 \\ +\ 3.7 \\ \hline \end{array}$	**7.** $\begin{array}{r} 2.5 \\ +\ 5.5 \\ \hline \end{array}$	**8.** $\begin{array}{r} 1.9 \\ +\ 5.6 \\ \hline \end{array}$	**9.** $\begin{array}{r} 1.0 \\ +\ 8.8 \\ \hline \end{array}$
10. $\begin{array}{r} 2.7 \\ +\ 6.3 \\ \hline \end{array}$	**11.** $\begin{array}{r} 3.7 \\ +\ 5.3 \\ \hline \end{array}$	**12.** $\begin{array}{r} 2.9 \\ +\ 1.0 \\ \hline \end{array}$	**13.** $\begin{array}{r} 8.6 \\ +\ 1.0 \\ \hline \end{array}$	**14.** $\begin{array}{r} 2.5 \\ +\ 1.7 \\ \hline \end{array}$

Find the differences.

15. $\begin{array}{r} 5.9 \\ -\ 2.5 \\ \hline \end{array}$	**16.** $\begin{array}{r} 1.3 \\ -\ 1.0 \\ \hline \end{array}$	**17.** $\begin{array}{r} 8.2 \\ -\ 6.3 \\ \hline \end{array}$	**18.** $\begin{array}{r} 7.4 \\ -\ 2.8 \\ \hline \end{array}$	**19.** $\begin{array}{r} 6.5 \\ -\ 1.6 \\ \hline \end{array}$
20. $\begin{array}{r} 4.7 \\ -\ 1.3 \\ \hline \end{array}$	**21.** $\begin{array}{r} 8.6 \\ -\ 4.2 \\ \hline \end{array}$	**22.** $\begin{array}{r} 9.3 \\ -\ 7.6 \\ \hline \end{array}$	**23.** $\begin{array}{r} 8.0 \\ -\ 6.8 \\ \hline \end{array}$	**24.** $\begin{array}{r} 7.6 \\ -\ 5.6 \\ \hline \end{array}$
25. $\begin{array}{r} 9.3 \\ -\ 6.8 \\ \hline \end{array}$	**26.** $\begin{array}{r} 3.0 \\ -\ 1.6 \\ \hline \end{array}$	**27.** $\begin{array}{r} 8.3 \\ -\ 7.2 \\ \hline \end{array}$	**28.** $\begin{array}{r} 9.4 \\ -\ 3.6 \\ \hline \end{array}$	**29.** $\begin{array}{r} 6.0 \\ -\ 1.5 \\ \hline \end{array}$

Name _____

Estimating the Answer

Before solving each problem, estimate the answer.
Then solve the problem and decide if your answer
is reasonable.

1. In New York City, 286 passengers
boarded the plane. In Atlanta,
the next stop, 112 more people
boarded the plane. How many
passengers are on the plane?

_____

2. Mark is flying to Boston with
his mother, father, and sister.
Adult tickets cost $286 each.
The children pay one half the
adult price. How much will plane
tickets cost for the whole family?

_____

Think about different strategies you can use. Then solve.

3. Lois can fly from Minneapolis
on a morning or afternoon flight.
She can take a plane that stops
in Chicago or Denver, or one
that does not stop at all. How
many choices does Lois have?

_____

4. A DC8-60 plane can carry 259
passengers. 8 people are waiting
to see if there will be room for
them on the plane. If 255 people
have tickets for that plane, and
2 of them do not come to the
airport, how many of the 8 will
be able to go on the plane?

_____

5. The flight attendants have served
lunch to $\frac{4}{7}$ of the passengers on
the plane. What fraction of the
passengers have not been
served yet?

_____

6. There are 9 lunch trays in each
section of the lunch cart. If the
cart holds 72 trays, how many
sections does it have?

_____

Name _____

Estimating Quotients Using Compatible Numbers

Find the quotients.

1. $2\overline{)12}$ **2.** $4\overline{)16}$ **3.** $3\overline{)18}$ **4.** $5\overline{)25}$

5. $5\overline{)15}$ **6.** $2\overline{)16}$ **7.** $4\overline{)32}$ **8.** $3\overline{)24}$

9. $3\overline{)12}$ **10.** $5\overline{)35}$ **11.** $2\overline{)14}$ **12.** $4\overline{)28}$

13. $4\overline{)20}$ **14.** $3\overline{)21}$ **15.** $5\overline{)15}$ **16.** $2\overline{)18}$

Estimate each quotient using compatible numbers.

17. $2\overline{)19}$ **18.** $3\overline{)16}$ **19.** $4\overline{)13}$ **20.** $5\overline{)29}$

21. $3\overline{)28}$ **22.** $4\overline{)23}$ **23.** $5\overline{)37}$ **24.** $3\overline{)19}$

25. $4\overline{)27}$ **26.** $5\overline{)14}$ **27.** $4\overline{)19}$ **28.** $3\overline{)19}$

29. $5\overline{)46}$ **30.** $3\overline{)20}$ **31.** $4\overline{)25}$ **32.** $4\overline{)31}$

33. $3\overline{)23}$ **34.** $5\overline{)34}$ **35.** $4\overline{)21}$ **36.** $5\overline{)39}$

Finding Quotients and Remainders: Making the Connection

Use counters and cups. Record what you do.
Find the quotient and remainder.

1. Divide 29 by 4.

How many cups will you use for the sharing? _____

How many counters are in each cup when you have shared

equally as many as possible? _____

How many of the counters were you able to use? _____

How many are left? _____

What is the quotient for 28 ÷ 4? _____

What is the remainder? _____

2. Divide 33 by 5. _____   **3.** Divide 44 by 5. _____

4. Divide 15 by 2. _____   **5.** Divide 26 by 5. _____

6. Divide 37 by 4. _____   **7.** Divide 17 by 3. _____

8. Divide 22 by 4. _____   **9.** Divide 27 by 4. _____

10. Divide 11 by 3. _____   **11.** Divide 34 by 5. _____

Dividing: Finding Quotients and Remainders

Divide. Find the quotients and remainders.

1. $5\overline{)36}$ **2.** $3\overline{)17}$ **3.** $3\overline{)23}$ **4.** $4\overline{)35}$

5. $3\overline{)24}$ **6.** $4\overline{)37}$ **7.** $3\overline{)22}$ **8.** $5\overline{)32}$

9. $3\overline{)19}$ **10.** $5\overline{)44}$ **11.** $2\overline{)9}$ **12.** $5\overline{)43}$

13. $5\overline{)3}$ **14.** $4\overline{)27}$ **15.** $2\overline{)13}$ **16.** $4\overline{)29}$

17. $3\overline{)26}$ **18.** $4\overline{)21}$ **19.** $3\overline{)29}$ **20.** $5\overline{)0}$

Checking Division

Find the quotients and remainders. Check your answers.

1. $3\overline{)25}$ **2.** $4\overline{)15}$ **3.** $2\overline{)19}$

4. $5\overline{)32}$ **5.** $3\overline{)14}$ **6.** $2\overline{)11}$

7. $5\overline{)28}$ **8.** $4\overline{)32}$ **9.** $4\overline{)18}$

Interpreting Remainders

Solve these problems. Think about
what the remainders mean.

1. Mary made jam for the county
fair. She used 4 peaches for
each jar. How many jars of jam
did she make with 35 peaches?

_____

2. Some children want to have
their faces painted. They have
30 tickets. It takes 4 tickets to
have one face painted. How
many children can have their
faces painted?

_____

3. 46 goats were brought to the
fair and put into pens. Each pen
holds 6 goats. How many pens
were needed?

_____

4. There are 72 lambs. Lambs are
judged in groups of 8. How
many groups of lambs will the
judges look at?

_____

5. Ken has 28 balloons. He sells
them in bunches of 3. How
many bunches can he sell?

_____

6. There are 44 plants. Each shelf
can hold 5 plants. How many
shelves are needed?

_____

7. 19 people want to ride the
Ferris wheel. Each seat holds
2 people. How many seats are
needed?

_____

8. Mandy has 19 tickets. A roller
coaster ride takes 6 tickets. How
many times can she go on the ride?

_____

Finding 2-Digit Quotients: Making the Connection

1. Use place value blocks. Start with 4 tens and 3 ones.
   Divide the blocks into 3 equal sets. Trade 1 ten for 10 ones as needed.

   When you have finished, how many are in each set? _____

   How many ones are left over? _____

   What is the quotient for 43 ÷ 3? _____

Use place value blocks to practice division with trading.

2. Divide 62 by 3.

   _____

3. Divide 41 by 4.

   _____

4. Divide 52 by 4.

   _____

5. Divide 32 by 3.

   _____

6. Divide 53 by 4.

   _____

7. Divide 62 by 5.

   _____

8. Divide 27 by 2.

   _____

9. Divide 67 by 5.

   _____

10. A box has 51 crackers. If 4 children share the crackers equally, how many will each child have? How many will be left over?

    _____

11. A package of paper has 64 sheets. If 5 children share the paper equally, how many sheets will each child have? How many will be left over?

    _____

Name _____

Estimating Money Quotients

Estimate the quotients. Decide if your
estimate is over or under.

1. $2.25 ÷ 2 _____ _____

2. $5.55 ÷ 2 _____ _____

3. $8.78 ÷ 3 _____ _____

4. $17.59 ÷ 6 _____ _____

5. $14.34 ÷ 7 _____ _____

6. $39.82 ÷ 5 _____ _____

7. $20.10 ÷ 4 _____ _____

8. $32.25 ÷ 8 _____ _____

9. $27.65 ÷ 7 _____ _____

10. $4.32 ÷ 2 _____ _____

11. $17.96 ÷ 3 _____ _____

12. $21.45 ÷ 7 _____ _____

13. $44.51 ÷ 5 _____ _____

14. $11.96 ÷ 4 _____ _____

15. $8.30 ÷ 4 _____ _____

16. $5.68 ÷ 3 _____ _____

17. $35.65 ÷ 6 _____ _____

18. $27.14 ÷ 9 _____ _____

19. $34.95 ÷ 5 _____ _____

20. $16.03 ÷ 4 _____ _____

21. $9.35 ÷ 3 _____ _____

22. $80.50 ÷ 9 _____ _____

23. $35.65 ÷ 4 _____ _____

24. $3.75 ÷ 4 _____ _____

25. $64.25 ÷ 8 _____ _____

26. $24.32 ÷ 3 _____ _____